The complete paintings of

Piero della Francesca

Introduction by **Peter Murray**

Notes and catalogue by **Pierluigi de Vecchi**

Harry N. Abrams, Inc.
Publishers, New York

**Classics of the
World's Great Art**

Editor
Paolo Lecaldano

**International
Advisory Board**
Gian Alberto dell'Acqua
André Chastel
Douglas Cooper
Lorenz Eitner
Enrique Lafuente Ferrari
Bruno Molajoli
Carlo L. Ragghianti
Xavier de Salas
David Talbot Rice
Jacques Thuillier
Rudolf Wittkower

*This series of books is
published in Italy by Rizzoli
Editore, in France by
Flammarion, in the United
Kingdom by Weidenfeld and
Nicolson, in the United States
by Harry N. Abrams, Inc.,
in Spain by Editorial
Noguer and in Switzerland by
Kunstkreis*

Standard Book Number 8109–5513–X
Library of Congress Catalogue
Card Number 78–85176
© Copyright in Italy by
Rizzoli Editore, 1967

Printed and bound in Italy

Table of contents

Introduction

Piero della Francesca, now probably the most popular of all fifteenth-century Italian artists, has only come to be appreciated in the last eighty years or so, but much of the appreciation that he now enjoys is rather beside the point. Ever since artists like Seurat endeavored to give back to painting something of the solidity and architectonic form which the Impressionists had rejected, there has been a tendency to regard Piero as a formal, monumental artist whose figures exist in their own right, as massively silent—and as meaningless—as the Pyramids. This point of view is reflected in the title of one of Berenson's last books, on Piero's "non-eloquent" art.

The rediscovery of Piero is partly due to artists like Seurat, but he was never as completely neglected as is sometimes claimed. By comparison with his Florentine predecessors and contemporaries we know little about the circumstances of his life, such as the date of his birth or the details of his training, but it is important to remember that he came from Sansepolcro, near Arezzo, and was thus born a Florentine citizen. Because Vasari himself came from Arezzo, he wrote a *Life* of his distinguished fellow Tuscan, and, indeed, claimed a rather distant connection with Piero. Sassetta and Giovanni di Paolo, Piero's great Sienese contemporaries, were neglected by Vasari because they were Sienese, and he does not even mention either of them. The *Life* by Vasari was, therefore, sufficient to ensure that Piero's name would be known to everybody interested in Italian painting, while the fact that his major work, the fresco cycle of *The Legend of the True Cross*, was in Arezzo and comparatively easy to see, means that it has not been necessary painfully to reconstruct his career from an investigation of documents coupled with the attribution of undocumented pictures on stylistic grounds.

In spite of Piero's Florentine citizenship, it seems clear that his earliest artistic education must have been overwhelmingly Sienese. Most of the pictures he knew in the cathedral and churches of his native Sansepolcro were by Sienese artists; and the altarpiece of St Francis of Assisi (most of which is now in the National Gallery, London) was begun by Sassetta for a church in Sansepolcro in 1437, when Piero was about twenty. Before this altarpiece was finished and erected, Piero had left Sansepolcro and is first recorded in Florence, working with another non-Florentine, Domenico Veneziano, on frescoes which have long since perished. This was in 1439, and soon afterwards Piero was back in Sansepolcro and starting an independent career which lasted into the 1470s, since he seems to have ceased painting long before his death in 1492. In the works of his earliest period, such as *The Baptism of Christ* in the National Gallery, Piero's own calm and simple style is already visible, but at the same time the feeling for pale, bright color, flat, even lighting, and grave, simple figures, reflect Sienese rather than Florentine taste. The work of Domenico Veneziano—which is particularly difficult to date—shares this disregard for the preoccupations of contemporary Florentine painters, and it is significant that on the only known occasion when Piero was working in Florence he collaborated with so untypical a Florentine painter. In fact, it is probable that this was not Piero's only visit to Florence, since it seems possible that he returned in the 1470s. By then he had become interested in the Flemish technique of oil painting, and it is likely that he studied the altarpiece in the Hospital in Florence (where he had himself worked in 1439), by the only Flemish artist of the late fifteenth century with a sense of scale comparable to Piero's own. This is the huge *Adoration of the Shepherds* painted by Hugo van der Goes for the Portinari family and presented by them to the Hospital about 1475.

Piero's style thus changed considerably, since his early works retain the pure, pale colors of traditional tempera painting and even the gold background which the Florentines had long abandoned, but which was

still common in Sienese pictures. We know that there was a Flemish painter active in Urbino when Piero was there in the 1470s, and he seems to have adopted the Flemish technique of painting oil-glazes over a tempera foundation more successfully than any other of his Italian contemporaries except Antonello da Messina. Nevertheless, although Piero's technique underwent great changes between an early work like *The Baptism of Christ* (Pls XIII & XVI) and a later one such as the Brera *Madonna with Duke Federico da Montefeltro* (Pl. LXIV), or the portraits of Federico and his duchess, yet his aesthetic ideals remained almost unaltered. He was one of the great exponents of perspective in the fifteenth century, and wrote a book on it, as well as a mathematical treatise in Latin. His use of perspective and foreshortening has none of the child-like naivety that we find in the work of his contemporary Uccello: on the contrary, it is used solely to create a credible picture space, fixed and defined, so that he can plot the positions of his figures in such a way that the harmonies of the composition are rigidly controlled by the imaginary world in which the figures stand. They stand rather than move, and because of this feeling for static composition rather than drama it has become a platitude to contrast Piero with his Florentine contemporaries interested in movement, anatomy, and dramatic expression. Indeed, if one compares Piero's *Brera Altarpiece* with an exactly contemporary Florentine work such as Antonio Pollaiuolo's *St Sebastian* in the National Gallery, London, it is evident that both men have a sense of pattern, both strive for the utmost realism in the setting, and both exploit the new technique of oil painting as far as they can. Yet the differences are far greater than the resemblances, and it is this which has led so many critics into thinking of Piero as a painter's painter, whose powers were concentrated exclusively upon pictorial ends, and who had no interest in the subject matter of his pictures.

Nothing can be further from the truth. There was no other painter active in the middle of the fifteenth century who was gifted to anything like the same extent as Piero in the invention of forms and colored shapes which, satisfying in themselves, also carry several layers of meaning. Some Florentine artists, such as Fra Filippo Lippi, in the series of *Madonnas* he painted in the 1450s and 1460s, contrive something very similar, and perhaps the greatest example in the whole century is the fusion of form and content in

Leonardo's *Last Supper*, painted a few years after Piero's death.

Examples of Piero's iconographical subtlety can be found in such pictures as *The Flagellation* (Pls VIII–X), *The Brera Altarpiece* (Pl. LXIV), and, above all, in his masterpiece, the cycle of frescoes of *The Legend of the True Cross*, painted for S. Francesco at Arezzo in the 1450s (Pls XIX–LII). This is perhaps the most striking example in Italian fifteenth-century painting of the importance of understanding the artist's intentions, since it is only when one is able to follow the complicated and elliptical narrative that one is able to appreciate the way in which Piero's forms grow out of his intention as a story-teller. Fortunately, it is possible to trace the sources of this narrative and so to reconstruct the intentions of Piero and of the donors of the cycle.

The Legend of the True Cross is a very rare subject. There are only two or three earlier examples, and two are, like Piero's, in Franciscan churches. The earliest (and largest to survive) is the series in the choir of the principal Franciscan church in Florence, Sta Croce, painted at the end of the fourteenth century by Agnolo Gaddi. The association with the Franciscans is not fortuitous, since the legend has a popular, dramatic quality rather like that of the *Meditations on the Life of Christ* written by a Franciscan in the late thirteenth century. The frescoes in Arezzo celebrate two Feasts of the Church, one in May commemorating the rediscovery or "Invention" in the early fourth century of the True Cross, and the other—the Exaltation of the Cross—in September. The Old and New Testament quotations used in the liturgy on these two days are, therefore, the starting-point for the narrative, but the Biblical texts were greatly expanded in *The Golden Legend*, written in the thirteenth century by Jacopo da Voragine, Bishop of Genoa. This collection of pious legends and edifying stories was one of the most popular books of the Middle Ages. Many of the stories are based on historical facts, but, as the author himself admits, the intention is edification rather than information; and it is this combination of history, the Old and New Testaments, and miracle stories, that makes it difficult for us to read Piero's narrative with the same ease as his contemporaries. Even for them, however, Piero's version would have been more difficult than Agnolo Gaddi's since he took it for granted that everybody knew the main outlines of the story, and he felt free to dispose the scenes in such a way

that they are paired, on opposite walls, like early medieval scenes from the Old and New Testaments—type and antitype—with the New Testament fulfilling the prophesies of the Old. Thus, for example, the two scenes at the top of each wall show Adam dying beneath a great tree (Pl XIX), and the return of the Cross to Jerusalem (Pls XLIX–LI); we are meant to read these together, so that we have the tree of the Fall, the tree which grew from Adam's grave and became Christ's Cross, and the Cross itself as the emblem of salvation—*Crux fidelis, inter omnes/Arbor una nobilis* . . . in the words of the Good Friday liturgy.

The same considerations apply to Piero's other works, and it has been shown that the *Brera Altarpiece*, with the mysterious egg suspended above the throne, has a symbolical meaning: so, too, has *The Flagellation* (Pls VIII–X), although there are still some iconographical oddities to be explained in it. Like a contemporary commentator on the Scriptures, Piero worked on several levels simultaneously, and the aesthetic is only one of the strands which go to make his work so much richer than that of most of his contemporaries. To look at the Arezzo frescoes as so much light, color, and volume is to gain a considerable aesthetic pleasure—but it is only a small part of what Piero meant us to experience.

PETER MURRAY

An outline of the artist's critical history

Before Vasari's eulogy—sincere no doubt, but chiefly prompted by civic pride—and apart from scanty praise from a few contemporaries, there are few references to Piero, and those few are devoted more to his theory of geometry than to his painting. This was true of the remaining years of the sixteenth century, but even admiration for him as a writer of treatises soon petered out. Over the next two centuries there was no mention of him, except an occasional dull echo of Vasari, and the first erudite notes on the artist by Arezzo-Urbino art historians (to them was due, especially in the early nineteenth century, the slowly awakening interest in the master), except for Lanzi's illuminating, brief outline. This was ignored by his immediate successors and not even acknowledged by Stendhal, so deeply indebted to Lanzi's *History*. Cicognara was an exception [1821, 1], but only in regard to Piero della Francesca as a student of perspective. For the rest, there is M. Valéry's passing reference to show to what a low ebb current ideas on the artist had fallen round about 1830, at the time of Von Rumohr's destructive criticism (a plodding, almost useless interpretation). It is true that Passavant immediately rejected it, but, in his turn, he saw in Piero nothing more than an industrious "primitive"; then there was Burckhardt, who traced the sources of his art to Squarcione of Padua. Only with James Dennistoun, just before the middle of the century, came the first enthusiastic support for genuine critical understanding. Immediately afterwards Piero's work began to appear in public collections. Not that his fame was undisputed; even in 1896 two illustrious art historians, Cavalcaselle and Morelli, gave a very low opinion of *The Flagellation* and *The Senigallia Madonna* (*Catalogue*, 11 and 27); and there was Rio's lack of understanding and the hesitations and uncertainties of many others, even amongst his most fervent admirers (Ch. Blanc [1870 and 1889], E. Müntz [1889], E. Marini-Franceschi [1911] etc.).

However, the "poetry of perspective" in Piero's work, singled out by Vischer in 1879, won over certain sensitive critics, above all Witting [1898] and Möller van den Bruck [1913]. Meanwhile a number of scholars brought to light biographical documents and texts relating to painting, esssential for the reconstruction of the artist's personality; and here Cavalcaselle may be mentioned again as having produced a well-balanced "catalogue" of the master, approved by Berenson himself.

In 1914 appeared Roberto Longhi's essay, in which Piero's style is defined as "a perspective synthesis of form and color," and Longhi defined the influence on Piero of the Florentine background, and his importance for the development of Antonello and Giambellino and many other fifteenth-century Ferrarese artists. Longhi's essay and his later writing were decisive for an understanding of Piero. Copies, too, of his frescoes at Arezzo (*Catalogue*, 15) played an important part as a stimulus to Seurat's "syncretism." Among numerous supporters and a few opponents Longhi's work gave rise to misunderstandings. He endeavored to overcome these by explaining that what he had written was not to be understood—as it had been by Lothe and others—in a cubistic sense, nor, as with Kurz [1955], as connected with surrealism, nor did it warrant drawing parallels between Piero and Corot, as Denis [1939] had done, nor justify seeing in the master a forerunner of abstract art, or of movements such as the "Golden Section" according to Rosenthal's ideas [1923] and those of some of his followers.

Later criticism confined itself to individual aspects of Piero's art. There was research into his symbols [Meiss, 1941 and 1954; Tolnay, 1955]; the identification of new paintings [Clark, 1947]; and general interpretations, such as that his art supplied a key to life at court, claimed by Hauser [1951], or to the common people, put forward by L. Venturi [1953]: contributions which in any case leave unaltered the critical edifice constructed by Longhi. His ideas remain all the more significant after the recent cleaning of the Arezzo frescoes which show that they are based on the "perspective synthesis of form and color."

Masaccio and Andrein [del Castagno], Paolo Uccello, Antonio and Pier [Pollaiuolo] such great artists, Piero of Borgo older than these . . .

G. SANTI, *Cronaca rimata*, after 1482

. . . Perspective, if one thinks of it, would be useless, were it not guided by geometry. This is fully shown by the Monarch of painting and architecture of our times, Pietro di Franceschi, our countryman, in his short treatise.

L. PACIOLI, *De Divina Proportione* (1497), 1509

. . . he was highly skilled in perspective, in which he was the master of Bramante, a cosmographer, a poet of the people and a fine painter.

SABBA DA CASTIGLIONE, *Ricordi overo Ammaestramenti*, 1554

[In the frescoes of San Francesco at Arezzo] there are many beautiful ideas and many figures worthy of praise; there are the dresses of the Queen of Sheba's women, painted in a charming new way, many lively and natural portraits, antique in style, a divinely measured row of Corinthian columns, and a serf leaning on his spade stands ready to hear St Helena speak, while the three Crosses are being dug up. The work could not be better done . . . But the most remarkable indication of his resource, judgment and art is his painting of an angle foreshortened . . . Piero shows in the obscurity how important it is to imitate reality and to draw from objects themselves. His great success has caused later artists to follow him and to attain that high level from which we now see things . . .

Piero was . . . a diligent student of his art who assiduously practiced perspective and had a thorough acquaintance with Euclid, so that he understood better than anyone else all the

curves in regular bodies and we owe to him the fullest light that has been thrown on the subject.

G.VASARI, *Le Vite*, 1568

. . . he was highly skilled in perspective and the greatest geometrician of his age, as is obvious from his books.

R.ALBERTI, *Trattato della Nobiltà della Pittura*, 1585

. . . he was supreme in mastering the difficulty of the regular bodies, in composition, arithmetic, geometry, perspective and painting . . . He illustrated beautiful and strange stories . . .

P.ORLANDI, *Abecedario pittorico*, 1719

. . . a painter to herald a new epoch in history. Apart from perspective, which he appears to have studied scientifically from its beginnings before any other Italian, painting owes much to his examples in imitating the effects of light, in tracing with intelligence the muscles of nudes, in preparing clay models of his figures, in the study of drapery, copied from the folds of the soft material with which he clothed them—and he liked to paint the folds very closely pressed together. Had he had the grace of Masaccio he would have been almost his equal . . . Moreover, in design, in atmosphere, in coloring his figures, one sees the beginning of that style which Piero Perugino carried further and Raphael perfected.

L.LANZI, *Storia pittorica della Italia*, 1795–96

. . . Piero della Francesca, a great Florentine artist of the fifteenth century, who lost his sight when he was thirty-four years old.

M.VALÉRY, *Voyages . . . en Italie*, 1831

These works [*The Flagellation* in Urbino, *The Resurrection* in Sansepolcro, *The Polyptych* in Perugia] reveal Piero's study of the paintings of Masaccio; for he not only gave them the same light effects, but imitated the light brown in certain flesh tones and the whitish tints in the shadows, a practice much praised in the Florentine master. His heads have something individual although they cannot be said to be beautiful, and (especially in tempera) he takes great care in painting the hair, which does not form a mass, but surrounds the face with long locks like ruffled wool. The figures are usually squat and sturdy, particularly the ankles which sometimes look swollen. Although the clothes are ample and sometimes swirling, the folds are rough and soft. The color is strong but less exaggerated than that used by most of his contemporaries. After what we have said about Piero's work, there is no need to contradict Rumohr's opinion in his *Italienischen Forschungen* [1827–31], that he was a most mediocre painter.

J.D.PASSAVANT, *Raffaello d'Urbino e il padre suo Giovanni Santi* (1839), 1882–91

These noble works, uniting a happy application of his favorite studies on perspective and light, with a grandeur and movement unknown to most of his compositions, are now mere wrecks, in which, however, may be traced not a few ideas subsequently appropriated by more celebrated artists. The most remarkable of them is *The Dream of Constantine*. In the play of light and the management of chiaroscuro, there is far more profound study than was usual among his contemporaries, and in no other work of so early a date have these been as successfully treated. By a not very intelligible juxtaposition, the companion compartment is occupied by an *Annunciation*, grave, solemn, almost severe, as are most of his later paintings. The lowest and largest space, on

either side of the choir, is filled by *The Battle*, whilst Constantine prays in a corner, surrounded by his courtiers. These may have suggested to Raffaele [Raphael] the same subject for the Stanze, but they afford no details calculated to animate his pencil. Soldiers, horses, and banners are, indeed, mingled together with a bustle and energy of action hitherto unattempted; but the effect is neutralized by an all-pervading confusion, and by a want of groups or episodes to concentrate the spectator's scattered interest or admiration. The design is generally good; the modeling and character of the heads are, as usual, excellent; the costumes are richly varied; and the horses remind us, by their action, of Pisano's pictures and medals.

J.DENNISTOUN, *Memoirs of the Dukes of Urbino*, 1851

His frescoes in S. Francesco at Arezzo . . . show such firm characterization, such movement and such luminous coloring that one is entirely unaware of the lack of a higher conception in the scenes portrayed. (Rumohr's belittling criticism remains for me inexplicable.)

J.BURCKHARDT, *Der Cicerone*, 1855

. . . it was not in the expression of contemplative ecstasy nor in religious pictures that Piero della Francesca's genius shone. Instead of these subjects, for which the vigorous and original qualities of his brush were insufficient, he had the vast and until then almost unexploited field of history. . . .

A.E.RIO, *L'Art Chrétien*, 1861

. . . in him was lacking above all the essential quality without which an artist cannot be amongst the finest, that is the choice of forms.

G.B.CAVALCASELLE–J.A.CROWE, *Storia della Pittura in Italia* (1864), 1898

Piero must be considered an important painter in the objective and the subjective sense. Objectively, because he possesses a comprehensive vision of painting: his figures are intimately connected with their background, and the painter never fails to take into consideration the proportion between zones of light and shadow before placing his figures in the composition. Subjectively, Piero shows greatness in that he uses matter as if he had to hollow it out of the hard ground in order to lay his foundations, as he cannot yet place himself on a plane of pure idealism: above all he wishes to be a realist, to draw in a realistic manner. The same care can be seen in the calm, clear composition of his pictures. In his larger works, in which he paints figures in groups—as in the frescoes in S. Francesco at Arezzo—he usually places them in a horizontal oval, as Masaccio did, but not with the intention of obtaining an absolute identification between formal and ideal content. On the contrary, from now onwards he begins to show a realistic aversion from special concentration of light.

R.VISCHER, *Luca Signorelli and the Italian Renaissance*, 1879

. . . he kept, though improving upon it, the traditional Greco-Roman type of the Sienese school, and, divesting it of a certain nebulosity in which Sienese art had restricted it, made the type more human, so that he prepared the way for the very beautiful work of the Umbrian school.

G.F.PICHI, *La Vita e le Opere di Piero della Francesca*, 1892

10

Impersonality—that is the quality whereby he holds us spell-bound, that is his most distinguishing virtue—one which he shares with only two other artists: the one nameless, who carved the pediments of the Parthenon, and the other Velasquez, who painted without ever betraying an emotion. . . . He was, however, impersonal not in his method only, as all great artists are, but he was what would be commonly called impassive, that is to say unemotional, in his conceptions as well. He loved impersonality, the absence of expressed emotion, as a quality in things. Having, for artistic reasons, chosen types the most manly, and, for perhaps similar reasons, a landscape which happens to be of the greatest severity and dignity, he combined and recombined them as each subject required, allowing the grand figures, the grand action, and the severe landscape, these, and these alone, to exercise upon us, as they must when all special emotion is disregarded, their utmost power. He never asks what his actors feel. Their emotions are no concern of his. Yet no "Flagellation" is more impressive than one of his, although you will not find on the face of any of the *dramatis personae* an expression responsive to the situation; and, as if to make the scene all the more severely impersonal, Piero has introduced into this marvellous picture three majestic forms who stand in the very foreground as unconcerned as the ever-lasting rocks . . .

The spell of an art as impersonal . . . is, I think, a compound of many things. In the first place, where there is no specialised ex-pression of feeling . . . we are left the more open to receive the purely artistic impressions of tactile values. . . . So unnecessary do I find facial expression, and indeed, at times so disturbing, that, if a great statue happens to be without a head, I seldom miss it; for the forms and the action, if both be adequate, are expressive enough to enable me to complete the figure. . .

B. BERENSON, *The Central Italian Painters of the Renaissance*, 1897

When confronted with his work, of a perfect and unchanging serenity, in which only the decorative harmony prevails, one has the impression that, in the second half of the fifteenth century, quivering as it was with life and passion, Piero has remained the last of the Primitives, an inheritor of Giotto and Angelico. He is, however, a Primitive who is not ignorant of the new scientific discoveries and, while using them without appearing to do so, subordinates everything to the rhythm of lines and colors.

A. PÉRATÉ, in *Histoire de l'Art* by A. Michel, 1908

Perspective, in its meaning of form, causes Piero to organize everything within the most simple and monumental outlines. It is as if every object must become one of the five regular bodies in order to serve the perspective construction. This construction is central, arranged on planes converging on an ideal axis, and by means of it Piero wants us to experience space as regular volume by placing in it other regular bodies. . . .

This determines the necessity for monumental human forms, statuesque and isolated poses, suspended gestures, all that com-plex of appearances which has been exchanged by psychological criticism for a sense of proud, heroic, hieratic impassivity. It would be easy to show that this is the inevitable outcome of his perspective vision.

His vision naturally requires a sense of static, fixed luminosity, either in bright sunlight or in artificial light—*The Baptism* in London or *The Dream of Constantine*—which must heighten form and color.

Thus Piero merges the problem of color with his other pictorial effects in such a way that almost every painting, having impressed us with a sense of profundity and of masses placed within the synthetic limits of straight lines and slight and ample curves, appears to us like a huge variegated intarsia; and this, on the lines of perspective planes, carries us to the surface by the continuity of the arrangement of his masses.

R. LONGHI, *Piero dei Franceschi e lo sviluppo della Pittura Veneziana*, in "L'Arte," 1913

Piero was inspired by the lucidity of genius in his examination of the achievements of art; for example, he sought with minute care the relationship that the formal elegant rhythms of the classicists might have—if they were subjected to any sort of reform—with the naturalness that Masaccio's world had earlier concealed. He was equally aware of the profound lesson enclosed in the inevitable landscape of the world created by Paolo Uccello, fascinated, at the same time, by the transfigured naturalness of Domenico's light, interested by Masolino's large but broken surfaces of color, and also in understanding the most minute and exquisite detail of painting, and attentive even to the recent insistence on the importance of line. He sought an art that would transmute poetically all these impulses into a strictly dis-posed universe whose melody should be broadly choral.

His most precious early discovery was a spontaneously archaic style. He discovered it at the very moment when he was con-templating the reform of classicism, and it is necessary to proceed with caution on how to understand this archaism. Was it an historical revival or something on which to fall back?

. . . We will restrict ourselves to considering this archaism as something to which Piero had recourse and which required no other explanation than that he was simply turning to certain subterranean perennial springs which rise to the surface in de-cisive moments to help artists eager for invention and lead them back to the main currents of figurative tradition.

R. LONGHI, *Piero della Francesca*, 1927

In Piero della Francesca's paintings, by the religious reverence for spatial intervals, by tonal and perspective organization, all movement, all rhythm, all plasticity itself, was translated equally into panorama terms.

A. LHOTE, in "La Nouvelle Revue Française," 1929

We hail in Piero della Francesca the first cubist. . . .

A. STOKES, *The Stones of Rimini*, 1929

. . . dramatic composition which is dissolving like shadows in light; tranquility in intelligible space.

H. FOCILLON, *Piero della Francesca* (1934–35), 1952

In him the spirit and the scientific mind were in harmony with the pictorial understanding of art and the search to exalt the solidity and stability of force and of the intimate. As a painter, he defined the volume of bodies and their relationships in space with such intensity as to present them as revelations, using for his purpose the most unstable elements: light and color; as a theorist he brought precision to mathematical severity. Color, even when diaphanous and brilliant, he understood as the covering of form. . . . Light did not co-ordinate the dramatic action, as it had with Masaccio and then with Andrea del Castagno; Piero did not see in it the quality of an ill-defined fluid as did Filippo Lippi, nor as dissolving plastic strength as

11

did Domenico Veneziano: he made of it the chief element in every appearance, seen for itself in its effect, neither fleeting nor instantaneous, but of a fixity which makes it more intense: devouring sunlight, light of the open sky, with deep transparences, giving brilliance to everything.

P. TOESCA, in "Enciclopedia Italiana," XXVII, 1935

. . . with Piero . . . form becomes the crystallization and the kernel of the spatial poem which develops in the fresco with incredible grandeur. Perspective which was mechanical becomes lyrical.

E. FAURE, L'Art Renaissant, 1939

Piero's color, which is all light, is for the first time so at one with form—ideally prepared to receive it—as to assume a plastic value, and this enables one to understand the unifying power of his art. By means of such complex stylistic work, form, the more abstract it becomes, so it loses movement and the outline of the figures loses linear sense—that is motion—being, as it were, generated as in a sphere by the turning of convex planes. And this absence of movement, this formidable ideal abstraction, disconcerts and frightens many people away from Piero della Francesca, for they cannot penetrate the meaning of an art in which the illustrative element is so subordinated to the stylistic element.

M. MARANGONI, Saper Vedere, 1942

Although deeply conscious of the prime factors in life and art, he is far from being primitive. He is, in the full, critical sense of the word, a classic artist, and to a large extent his rediscovery was part of a new classicism, of which Cézanne and Seurat were the living manifestations. It is not surprising that the admirers of Cézanne took a different view of quattro-cento art from the admirers of Burne-Jones. They were looking not for fantasy, but for order; not for grace, but for solidity. The word "blocks," applied to Piero's figures as a term of reproach by Crowe and Cavalcaselle, became a term of praise in the new concept of pictorial architecture. In particular Piero's application of geometry, not only to whole compositions but to individual figures, was in harmony with the spirit which was later to find expression in Cubism and its derivatives.

K. CLARK, Piero della Francesca, 1951

The deification of man is the triumph of humanism and thus Piero's altarpiece (Brera, Milan) synthesizes spiritual civilization in the fifteenth century. The steady, fixed light in the museum partly destroys some of the variations and vibrations of that enchanting silvery light bathing the architecture and, here and there, touching the figures; only those who have seen Piero's work in a good light can have an idea of what a miracle it is. But the most unobservant visitor will realize that this altarpiece is far superior to any Florentine design, that Piero della Francesca's exceptionally beautiful masses are obtained by condensation in plastic planes, and the whole atmosphere is a tissue of mysterious ethereal colors. The sublimation of Piero della Francesca's genius moves us. It is enriched by the most lofty science and philosophy of the Renaissance, an affirmation of the most absolute intellectuality, intoning, on the eve of death, a pure, lyrical song.

F. WITTGENS, La Pala Urbinate di Piero, 1952

Piero's love of ornate, oriental costumes, fantastic head-dresses, the trappings of tournaments, was shared by the people. . . . But the way in which this is revealed in his paintings shows how Piero insinuated a corrective into the popular taste for display and luxury: irony. Irony puts in a fleeting appearance in this or that detail, shows the artist's detachment from his theme and wonderfully allies itself with the geometrical abstraction of his forms. Irony and abstract concepts form a screen, even if transparent, between the artist and reality; although Piero can be a realist in his own way. . . .

L. VENTURI, Piero della Francesca, 1954

Ritual solemnity is characteristic of all Piero's compositions. His figures never seem to perform a transient action in this world, nor to take part in any real event; they appear immersed in a sacred cult with slow and solemn gestures, sometimes with serious, impassive expression, sometimes with serene piety. They all seem to be interpreting a scene from the divine Mystery and celebrating absolute Truth. Their life is protected from all surprise.

Such freedom from cares and the simplification of the souls of Piero's characters permits the artist, as well as the spectator, to concentrate on the effects produced by form, color, and line; the masses in the form of cubes and cones, the decorative shapes, seen front-view and in profile, which receive his sunlit, shadowless colors, the beauty of curious, skillful overlapping, all create an enchanted kingdom of imperishable forms and pure colors. It is as if one had soared into a world of archetypes.

CH. DE TOLNAY, La Résurrection du Christ par Piero della Francesca, in "Gazette des Beaux-Arts," 1954

This "monarch of painting," according to Pacioli's expression, was for the generation of the middle of the century a personality as complete as that of Giotto and like him of national not provincial character. The beautiful small picture of The Flagellation reveals that precise clarity based on strict perspective which is less cramped than Uccello's. Piero's geometrical intuition and the intensity of his colors are raised equally to the highest degree of effectiveness, transforming the universe into a luminous cage, without chinks, where humanity cannot stray. . . . The impersonality of this art creates its nobility, but it is qualified by two aspects, one rustic, countrified, evident in the types, the other noble, heroic, legendary, and their meeting perhaps explains the epic accent of the work. This is certainly true of the Arezzo cycle.

A. CHASTEL, L'Art Italien, 1956

Alberti shows himself as retrograde in maintaining that the sole aim of painting is the representation of objects and surfaces. For Alberti, a follower of Brunelleschi and Manetti, surfaces are to be considered henceforward as the meeting place of planes in space. But in eliminating from painting everything not directly visible from an angle adopted for a so-called unitary representation, Alberti considerably reduces the scope of his doctrine. The best proof of this is that all painters have not followed him. Piero attaches enormous importance to geometrical construction and projection from surfaces, but is not the essence of his genius the way in which he makes masses more sensitive, and reveals the heavy realities concealed beneath the apparent surfaces of objects firmly fixed by the rigid point of view advocated by Alberti?

P. FRANCASTEL, Peinture et Société, 1957

He causes everything, in a mysterious system of reciprocal attraction, to unite to create a solid hermetic world made abstract by the purifying geometry of forms and by light without vibrations, in which gravity adheres to an elementary reality. A world in which live—classless and motionless and without apparent emotions—beings equally removed from human tragedy and divine beatitude, these same primordial elements of reality—trees, mountains, architecture—substitute for moral law the religion of measure and harmony. A limbo without guilt and without sanctity, where mystery and certainty merge in the same rhythmic equilibrium which, arresting every gesture, calms all feeling. An immaculate and limitless dominion of structural solidity arranged in a slow sacerdotal gravity.

Nothing disturbs the bloodless serenity of this planet: not the passions (his beings are purified of them), not the mind of its creator, on the alert not to interfere, not to impose his own emotions, but rather to arouse in us the same forces which have been aroused in him. Yet no artist—without pathetic appeal, without recourse to sentimental means, restricting himself to a scrupulous impersonality—has ever achieved work so complex, so absolute, so valid, so convincing; no artist has ever found a grander, more changeless kingdom, which the rule of order and poetry have raised to the solitary heaven of perfection.

P. LECALDANO, *I Grandi Maestri della Pittura Italiana del Quattrocento*, 1958

The mediation between "man" and "nature" or, expressed in figurative terms, between "form" and "color" was realized by perspective, a discovery whose significance Piero appreciated in Florence, either through the study of Masaccio's works or by frequenting Brunelleschi's milieu. And it was this discovery that fired his imagination, made him see in nature what others had not seen, nourished the supreme calm typical of his work, and led him to record in extremely rigorous treatises the date of his geometrical and mathematical experiences. "A perspective synthesis of form and color" is the phrase Longhi used to pinpoint the motionless and spectacular perfection of Piero's art, where the luminous intuition was translated into forms of solemn and pondered greatness. It is a formula which, in its brevity, while it throws light on the artist's intimate and complex experiences, gives the meaning of their lucid change into the eternal substance of a language as revolutionary and positive as that of a Giotto or a Masaccio, but, with the passing of time, gives a glimpse of a greater vision.

S. BOTTARI, in "Encyclopedia of World Art," XI, 1959

The art of Piero has been compared with the music of Mozart and the poetry of Wordsworth. But his ability to embrace the world at a glance can also be compared with Tolstoy's faculty of admiring in *War and Peace* the curve of a comely prostitute's shoulders and bowing before the peasant Karataiev's wisdom. Piero has no need of tiresome didacticism, nor of rhetoric; he affects and enchants us by bringing us face to face with the real problems of human beings. . . .

Alberti's expression "circumscription" is inaccurate to describe Piero's draftsmanship. Each object approaches as nearly as possible to the regular bodies by which, according to Vasari, the artist was attracted. At the same time the dynamism of his line shares in the design. Alberti only admired it in the waving hair of women. Thanks to the dynamism of his line, Piero not only outlines static objects but also conveys their inherent static force.

M. ALPATOV, *Les Fresques de Piero della Francesca à Arezzo—Sémantique et Stylistique*, in "Commentari," 1963

The Paintings in Color

List of plates

In the captions beneath the color plates the height and width of each picture — or the part which is reproduced — is given (in centimeters)

PLATE I   POLYPTYCH OF THE MISERICORDIA   Sansepolcro, Town Hall
The Crucifixion (52.5 cm.)

PLATE II   POLYPTYCH OF THE MISERICORDIA   Sansepolcro, Town Hall
St Benedict of Norcia and *The Angel of the Annunciation* (21 and 20.5 cm. respectively)

PLATE III POLYPTYCH OF THE MISERICORDIA Sansepolcro, Town Hall
The Virgin Annunciate and *St Francis* (each 21 cm.)

PLATE IV   POLYPTYCH OF THE MISERICORDIA   Sansepolcro, Town Hall
St Sebastian and *St John the Baptist* (90 cm. overall)

PLATE V POLYPTYCH OF THE MISERICORDIA Sansepolcro, Town Hall
St Andrew and *St Bernardino of Siena* (90 cm. overall)

PLATE VI   POLYPTYCH OF THE MISERICORDIA Sansepolcro, Town Hall
The Madonna of the Misericordia (134 cm.)

PLATE VII   POLYPTYCH OF THE MISERICORDIA Sansepolcro, Town Hall
Detail of the worshipers in *The Madonna of the Misericordia* (45 cm.)

OPVS·PETRI·DE·BVRGO·SCI·SEPVLCRI

PLATES VIII-IX   THE FLAGELLATION OF CHRIST Urbino, National Gallery of the Marches
Whole (81.5 cm.)

PLATE X   THE FLAGELLATION OF CHRIST Urbino, National Gallery of the Marches
Detail of the first figure on the right (uncertain identification) life size

PLATE XI ST JEROME IN PENITENCE Berlin, Staatliche Museen
Whole (38 cm.)

PLATE XII ST JEROME AND A WORSHIPER Venice, Accademia
Whole (42 cm.)

PLATE XIII   THE BAPTISM OF CHRIST   London, National Gallery
Whole (116 cm.)

PLATE XIV THE BAPTISM OF CHRIST London, National Gallery
Detail of Christ (life size)

PLATE XV THE BAPTISM OF CHRIST London, National Gallery
Detail (life size)

PLATE XVI   THE BAPTISM OF CHRIST London, National Gallery
Details (32.5 cm. each)

PLATE XVII   ST SIGISMUND AND SIGISMONDO PANDOLFO MALATESTA   Rimini, Tempio Malatestiano
Whole (285 cm.) and detail (142 cm.)

PLATE XVIII   THE "MADONNA DEL PARTO" Monterchi (Arezzo), Cemetery Chapel
Whole (203 cm.)

PLATE XIX   THE LEGEND OF THE TRUE CROSS   Arezzo, Church of S. Francesco
Details of *The Death of Adam* (above, 200 cm., below 55 cm.)

PLATES XX-XXI   THE LEGEND OF THE TRUE CROSS Arezzo, Church of S. Francesco
The Adoration of the True Cross and King Solomon's Meeting with the Queen of Sheba (747 cm.)

PLATE XXII   THE LEGEND OF THE TRUE CROSS Arezzo, Church of S. Francesco
Detail of a groom from *The Adoration of the True Cross* (55 cm.)

PLATE XXIII THE LEGEND OF THE TRUE CROSS Arezzo, Church of S. Francesco
Detail of the Queen of Sheba from *The Adoration of the True Cross* (55 cm.)

PLATE XXIV   THE LEGEND OF THE TRUE CROSS Arezzo, Church of S. Francesco
Detail of the Queen of Sheba's retinue from *The Adoration of the True Cross* (90 cm.)

PLATE XXV   THE LEGEND OF THE TRUE CROSS Arezzo, Church of S. Francesco
Detail of the court dignitaries of the king from *King Solomon's Meeting with the Queen of Sheba* (90 cm.)

PLATE XXVI   THE LEGEND OF THE TRUE CROSS   Arezzo, Church of S. Francesco
Detail of the two sovereigns from *King Solomon's Meeting with the Queen of Sheba* (70 cm.)

PLATE XXVII   THE LEGEND OF THE TRUE CROSS Arezzo, Church of S. Francesco
Detail of the queen's women from *King Solomon's Meeting with the Queen of Sheba* (55 cm.)

PLATE XXVIII THE LEGEND OF THE TRUE CROSS Arezzo, Church of S. Francesco
The Annunciation (193 cm.)

PLATE XXIX   THE LEGEND OF THE TRUE CROSS Arezzo, Church of S. Francesco
Detail of the Virgin in *The Annunciation* (53 cm.)

PLATE XXX   THE LEGEND OF THE TRUE CROSS Arezzo, Church of S. Francesco
The Torture of the Jew (193 cm.)

PLATE XXXI   THE LEGEND OF THE TRUE CROSS Arezzo, Church of S. Francesco
Detail from *The Torture of the Jew* (35 cm.)

PLATE XXXII   THE LEGEND OF THE TRUE CROSS Arezzo, Church of S. Francesco
Detail from *The Dream of Constantine* (130 cm.)

PLATE XXXIII   THE LEGEND OF THE TRUE CROSS Arezzo, Church of S. Francesco
Detail of *The Battle between Constantine and Maxentius* (90 cm.)

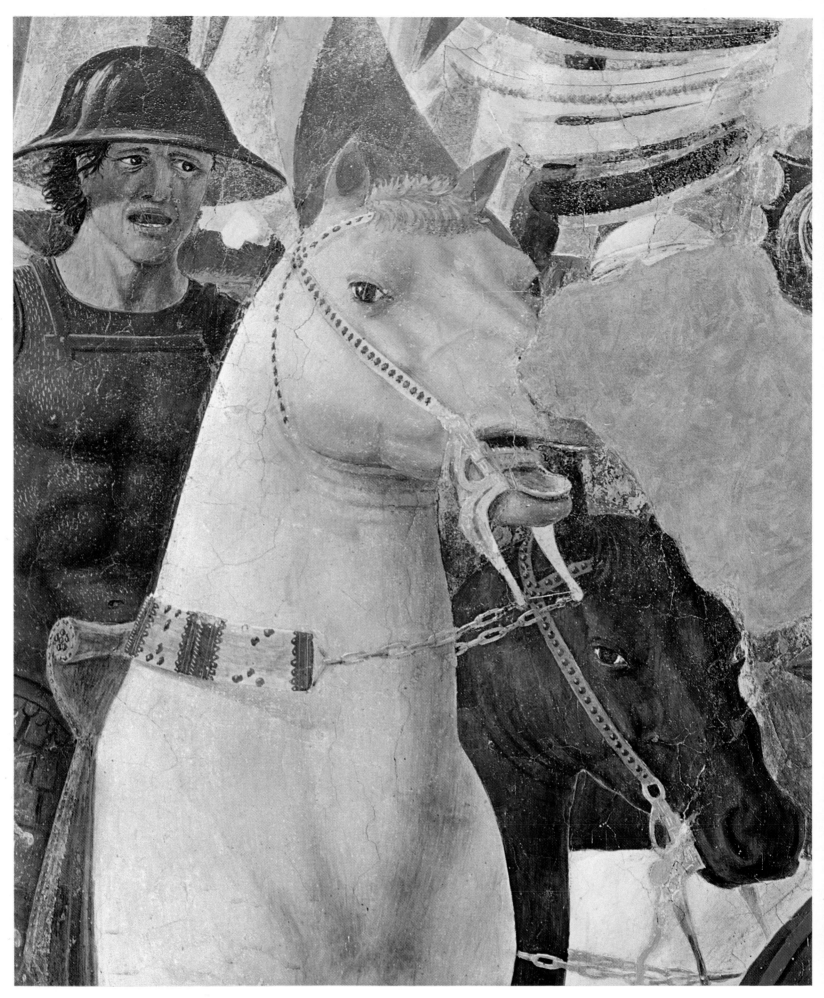

PLATE XXXIV   THE LEGEND OF THE TRUE CROSS   Arezzo, Church of S. Francesco
Detail of *The Battle between Constantine and Maxentius* (90 cm.)

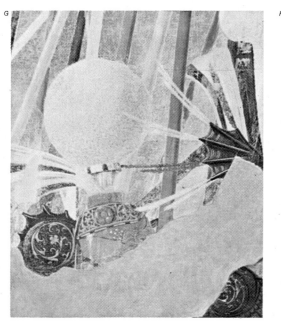

PLATE XXXV   THE LEGEND OF THE TRUE CROSS Arezzo, Church of S. Francesco
Details of *The Battle between Constantine and Maxentius* (each 70 cm.)

PLATE XXXVIII   THE LEGEND OF THE TRUE CROSS   Arezzo, Church of S. Francesco
Detail of *The Discovery of the Three Crosses* (143 cm.)

PLATE XXXIX   THE LEGEND OF THE TRUE CROSS   Arezzo, Church of S. Francesco
Detail of *The Discovery of the Three Crosses* (143 cm.)

PLATE XL   THE LEGEND OF THE TRUE CROSS Arezzo, Church of S. Francesco
Detail of Jerusalem from *The Discovery of the Three Crosses* (125 cm.)

PLATE XLII   THE LEGEND OF THE TRUE CROSS Arezzo, Church of S. Francesco
St Helena and her suite from *The Proving of the True Cross* (143 cm.)

PLATE XLIII   THE LEGEND OF THE TRUE CROSS   Arezzo, Church of S. Francesco
The Resurrection of the Young Man from *The Proving of the True Cross* (143 cm.)

PLATES XLIV-XLV   THE LEGEND OF THE TRUE CROSS   Arezzo, Church of S. Francesco
The Battle between Heraclius and Chosroes (747 cm.)

THE LEGEND OF THE TRUE CROSS Arezzo, Church of S. Francesco
Detail from *The Battle between Heraclius and Chosroes* (70 cm.)

PLATE XLVII   THE LEGEND OF THE TRUE CROSS Arezzo, Church of S. Francesco
Detail from *The Battle between Heraclius and Chosroes* (185 cm.)

PLATE XLIX   THE LEGEND OF THE TRUE CROSS Arezzo, Church of S. Francesco
The Exaltation of the Cross: whole (747 cm.) and detail (500 cm.)

PLATE L   THE LEGEND OF THE TRUE CROSS   Arezzo, Church of S. Francesco
Detail from *The Exaltation of the Cross* (260 cm.)

PLATE LI   THE LEGEND OF THE TRUE CROSS Arezzo, Church of S. Francesco
Detail from *The Exaltation of the Cross* (260 cm.)

PLATE LII   THE LEGEND OF THE TRUE CROSS Arezzo, Church of S. Francesco
Prophet (90 cm.)

PLATE LIII

ST MARY MAGDALEN Arezzo, Cathedral
Whole (100 cm.)

PLATE LIV

PLATE LIV

THE POLYPTYCH OF ST AUGUSTINE   Lisbon, Museu de Arte Antiga
St Augustine (60 cm.)

THE POLYPTYCH OF ST ANTONY Perugia, National Gallery of Umbria
The Annunciation (194 cm.)

PLATE LVIII   THE POLYPTYCH OF ST ANTONY Perugia, National Gallery of Umbria
Details from *The Annunciation* (each 25 cm.)

PLATE LIX   THE RESURRECTION OF CHRIST Sansepolcro, Town Hall
Whole (200 cm.)

PLATE LX   THE DIPTYCH OF THE DUKE AND DUCHESS OF URBINO   Florence, Uffizi
Portrait of Battista Sforza (33 cm.)

PLATE LXI THE DIPTYCH OF THE DUKE AND DUCHESS OF URBINO Florence, Uffizi
Portrait of Federico II da Montefeltro (33 cm.)

CLARVS INSIGNI VEHITVR TRIVMPHO ·
QVEM PAREM SVMMIS DVCIBVS PERHENNIS ·
FAMA VIRTVTVM CELEBRAT DECENTER ·
SCEPTRA TENENTEM

PLATE LXII   THE DIPTYCH OF THE DUKE AND DUCHESS OF URBINO Florence, Uffizi
Triumph of Federico II da Montefeltro (33 cm.)

QVE MODVM REBVS TENVIT SECVNDIS ·
CONIVGIS MAGNI DECORATA RERVM ·
LAVDE GESTARVM VOLITAT PER ORA ·
CVNCTA VIRORVM ↜

PLATE LXIII   THE DIPTYCH OF THE DUKE AND DUCHESS OF URBINO Florence, Uffizi
Triumph of Battista Sforza (33 cm.)

PLATE LXIV   THE BRERA ALTARPIECE   Milan, Brera
Whole (170 cm.)

The works

Key to symbols used

In order to make the principal particulars about each painting immediately clear, after each number there is a heading. The pictures are numbered in what is their generally accepted chronological order and the number is quoted every time the work is mentioned in the book. After the number there follows a series of symbols referring: 1 to the execution of the painting, that is the proof of its authenticity; 2 the technique; 3 whether it is on wood, wall, or canvas; 4 its location; 5 other information: whether the work is signed, dated, whether it is complete in all its parts, whether it is finished. The other numbers forming part of each heading refer—those on the upper line—to the size of the painting in centimeters (height and width). When the date cannot be given with certainty, but only approximately, it is preceded and/or followed by an asterisk * according to whether the uncertainty relates to the period preceding the indicated date, that following, or both. All the information gives the prevailing opinion in present day history of art: every important disagreement and every former attribution is stated in the text.

EXECUTION

Original work

With assistants

In collaboration

Mostly the work of collaborators

From Piero's studio

Generally attributed to Piero

Attribution to Piero generally rejected

Traditionally attributed to Piero

Recently attributed to Piero

Technique

Oil

Fresco

Tempera

Support

Panel

Wall

Canvas

Location

Open to public

Private collection

Whereabouts unknown

Lost

Additional information

Signed

Dated

Incomplete or fragmentary

Unfinished

Information given in the text

LIST OF ABBREVIATIONS

A: *L'Arte* (Rome—Turin—Milan)
AA: *Art in America* (Springfield—New York)
AAL: *Atti della R. Accademia dei Lincei* (Rome)
AB: *The Art Bulletin* (Washington—Providence)
AC 1912: *Atti del X Congresso internazionale di Storia dell'arte in Roma, 1912* (Rome 1922)
ACHA: *Actes du XVIIème Congrès international d'Histoire de l'art* (The Hague 1955)
ACSS: *Atti del Congresso internazionale di scienze storiche in Roma, 1904* (Rome 1905)
AS: *Arte e storia* (Florence)
ASA: *Archivio storico dell'Arte* (Rome)
AZK: *Archiv für die zeichnenden Künste mit besonderer Rücksicht auf Kupferstecher und Holzschneidekunst und ihre Geschichte* (Leipzig)
B: *Il Buonarroti* (Rome)
BA: *Bollettino d'Arte* (Rome)

BEA: *Belle Arti* (Pisa)
BICR: *Bollettino dell'Istituto centrale del restauro* (Rome)
BM: *The Burlington Magazine* (London)
C: *Corvina* (Florence)
CA: *La Critica d'Arte* (Florence)
CCE: *Cronache della Civiltà Elleno-Latina* (Rome)
CDS: *Corriere della Sera* (Milan)
CM: *Commentari* (Florence)
CN: *Classici Neolatini* (Aosta)
CO: *The Connoisseur* (London)
D: *Dedalo* (Milan)
GBA: *Gazette des Beaux-Arts* (Paris)
GNI: *Le Gallerie Nazionali Italiane* (Rome)
HK: *Handbuch der Kunstwissenschaft* (Berlin)
JPK: *Jahrbuch der Preussischen Kunstsammlungen* (Berlin)
JWCL: *Journal of the Warburg and Courtauld Institutes* (London)
LM: *Le Marche* (Fano-Senigallia)
M: *Marsyas* (New York)
NRM: *Nuova Rivista Misena* (Arcevia)

P: *Paragone* (Florence)
R: *Rinascimento* (Florence—Rome)
RA: *Rassegna d'Arte* (Milan)
RAL: *Rendiconti dell'Accademia Nazionale dei Lincei* (Rome)
RAU: *Rassegna d'Arte Umbra* (Perugia)
RC: *Il Resto del Carlino* (Bologna)
RDA: *Rivista d'Arte* (Florence)
RFK: *Repertorium für Kunstwissenschaft* (Berlin—Leipzig)
RI: *Rivista d'Italia* (Milan)
RT: *La Rinascita* (Florence)
SBA: *Sitzungsberichte der Bayerischen Akademie der Wissenschaften* (Munich)
SDCG: *Studies in Art and Literature for Belle Da Costa Green* (Princeton 1954)
T-B: *Allgemeines Lexikon der Bildenden Künstler* of U. Thieme and F. Becker (Leipzig)
VA: *Vasari* (Florence)
ZFBK: *Zeitschrift für Bildende Kunst* (Leipzig)

Bibliography

A bibliographical index on Piero, almost complete up to 1926, can be found in the important monograph by R. Longhi [*Piero della Francesca*, Milan 1927], improved in its second edition and brought up to 1962 in his essay in "Paragone" [1963] and then in the third edition of the monograph [Florence 1964]. U. Baldini, too [in *Mostra di quattro maestri del primo Rinascimento*, Florence 1954], made a great contribution to Piero's bibliography. Among the most distinguished works, apart from G. Vasari [*Le Vite*, Florence 1550 and 1568 (edited by C.L. Ragghianti, Milan—Rome 1942–9)] and the notes of L. Lanzi [*Storia pittorica della Italia*, Bassano 1795–6, English edition; *History of Painting in Italy*, translated by Roscoe 1828 (Vol. 1 on Florence and Siena) in 1847 in 3 vols.], are the following: J.A. Crowe and G.B. Cavalcaselle [*History of Painting in Italy*, London 1864–6 (and the German edition, Leipzig 1870, and the Italian edition, Florence 1898)], B. Berenson [*Central Italian Painters of the Renaissance*, London 1897, 1909, and 1911; *Italian Pictures of the Renaissance*, Oxford 1932 and 1953; *Piero della Francesca o dell'Arte non eloquente*, Florence 1950 (English edition available); *Italian Pictures of the Renaissance*, 3 vols., newly revised and illustrated, 1968 (*The Central Italian and North Italian Pictures of the Renaissance*.)], F. Witting [*Piero dei Franceschi*, Strasbourg 1898], W. G. Waters [*Piero della Francesca*, London 1901, A. Venturi [*History of Art* VII i, Milan 1911; *Piero della Francesca*, Florence 1922], Möller van den Bruck [*Die italienische Schönheit*, Munich 1913], R. van Marle [*The Development of the Italian Schools of Painting*, XI, The Hague 1929], P. Toesca [in "Enciclopedia Italiana," XXVII, Milan—Rome 1935], M. Meiss [AB (for this and similar abbreviations see below) 1941; ACHA], C.E. Gilbert [M 1941], M. Salmi [*Piero della Francesca e il Palazzo Ducale di Urbino*, Florence 1945; R 1958; *Pittura e miniatura a Ferrara nel primo Rinascimento*, Milan 1961; *Piero della Francesca . . . Le Storie della Croce* (in the series "Forma e Colore") Florence 1965], J. Alazard [*Piero della Francesca*, Paris 1948], A. Stokes [*Art and Science—a study of Alberti, Piero della Francesca, and Giorgione*, London 1949], R. Longhi [as well as the above-mentioned and his

authoritative essay on *Piero dei Franceschi e lo sviluppo della Pittura Veneziana* (A 1914); P 1950; *Piero della Francesca. The Legend of the Cross*, Milan 1951 and 1955], K. Clark [*Piero della Francesca*, London 1951], M. Davies [National Gallery Catalogues—*The Earlier Italian Schools*, London 1951 and 1961], E. Gombrich [review of K. Clark's monograph on Piero in "The Burlington Magazine", London 1952; pp. 176–8], X. Lauts [article on the lost Ferrarese frescoes, "The Burlington Magazine", London 1953], L. Venturi [*Piero della Francesca*, Geneva 1954], P. Bianconi [*All the Paintings of Piero della Francesca*, Milan 1957, 1959, and 1964], S. Bottari [in "Encyclopedia of World Art", XI, Venice—Rome, New York, Toronto, London 1959–], A. Busignani [*Piero della Francesca*, 1967], and P. Hendy [*Piero della Francesca and the Early Italian Renaissance*, London and New York, 1968].

In regard to theoretical work (see *Appendix*), first of all works by Piero della Francesca are given: *De Prospectiva Pingendi* (known from two manuscripts: n. 1576 in the Palatinate Library in Parma, the Italian text and the designs both in Piero's hand; and C. 307 inf. in the Ambrosiana Library in Milan with the text translated into Latin by Matteo del Borgo in a scribe's hand, but with corrections and designs by Piero himself; the first was published with scrupulous care by G. Nicco Fasola [Florence 1942]; the second by C. Winterberg [Strasbourg 1899]), *Libellus de quinque corporibus regularibus* (Cod. Urbinate 632 in the Vatican Library, in a copyist's hand with designs drawn by Piero; published by G. Mancini [RAL 1915]) and *Del abaco* (Cod. Ashb. 359 of the Laurentian Library of Florence, by a copyist); then the works of L. Pacioli: *Summa Arithmeticae* [Venice 1494] and *De Divina Proportione* [Venice 1509]. Lastly one must mention the studies of: M. Jordan [JPK 1880], G. Pittarelli [ACSS], E. Panofsky [Durers *Kunsttheorie*, Berlin 1915], L. Olschki [*Geschichte der neusprachlichen wissenschaftlichen Literatur*, 1918], J. Schlosser-Magnino [*La letteratura artistica*, Florence 1935, 1956, and 1964], A. Guzzo [*La scienza*, Turin 1955] and A. Parronchi [*Studi su la dolce prospettiva*, Milan 1964].

Outline biography

1415–20 Piero was probably born at Borgo San Sepolcro (today Sansepolcro) near Arezzo during this period. His father, a shoemaker and leather-dresser, was called Benedetto de' Franceschi, his mother Romana di Perino da Monterchi. The date usually given for his birth lies between 1410 (near to 1406 claimed by Vasari) and 1420; Ragghianti points out that since he does not yet appear in 1439 (see below) as independent master, it would be more logical to fix the date about 1420. Already in the past the name "de' Franceschi" had changed to "della Francesca," by which Piero is generally known; the reason for the change remains unknown. Vasari's explanation cannot be accepted: "he was called after his mother 'Della Francesca' because she was with child when his father died."

1430 The little-known master Antonio d'Anghiari received a commission to paint an altarpiece for the church of S. Francesco at Borgo San Sepolcro which, seven years later, was entrusted to Sassetta. It is possible that Piero could have learnt the rudiments of his art from the almost contemporary Antonio.

c. **1435** Longhi thinks that Piero was apprenticed in Florence to Domenico Veneziano (see under **1439**) and that the young man then accompanied the master to the Marches (where Vasari records his collaboration in the frescoes in the Sacristy of Loreto) and to Umbria (where Domenico's stay is proved by a letter from him addressed to Piero de' Medici in 1438).

1439 7 September The Sta Maria Nuova hospital in Florence paid Domenico Veneziano for the frescoes in the choir of Sant' Egidio; in the relevant document is recorded: "Pietro di Benedetto dal Borgo a San Sepolcro" as assisting with the work under Domenico ("who is [with him]").

1442 He is mentioned again at Borgo San Sepolcro as one of the city councillors.

1445 11 January The Confraternity of the Misericordia of Borgo San Sepolcro commissioned him to paint a large polyptych for the altar of their church; as was the custom of the time, the contract stipulated the quality of the paints and of the gold, that it must be his own work and the date by which it must

 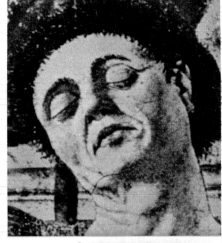

Presumed self-portraits of Piero della Francesca from the central part of the Polyptych of the Misericordia (Catalogue, 7) *and the* Resurrection *at Sansepolcro* (19).

be finished (during 1448). Because of the unevenness of the work, his having had recourse to assistants and the lateness in handing it over (see **1462**; and *Catalogue* 7 A-H) it is inferred that the young painter's stay in his native town was not prolonged much after 1445, perhaps because at about that time his relationship began with the Duke of Urbino, Federico II da Montefeltro, who had recently

succeeded his brother Oddantonio, assassinated in July 1444. If *The Flagellation* at Urbino (*Catalogue* 11) is linked with that violent death, it seems reasonable to suppose such an early beginning of the relationship [Longhi].

c. **1450** He worked in Ferrara, carrying out frescoes (lost) in the Estense Castle and in the church of Sant'Agostino. The date is inferred from records of such works which probably echoed Ferrarese miniatures of 1448 [Salmi]; in any case modern scholars agree on the middle of the century (or 1449) and are unanimous in recognizing the importance of Piero's work in the later development of painting in the Emilian city.

1450 This date is written on *St Jerome in Penitence* in Berlin. (*Catalogue* 8).

1451 This date appears on the fresco of Sigismondo Malatesta kneeling before his patron saint at Rimini (*Catalogue* 10). The journeys of Piero from Urbino to Ferrara and to Rimini coincided with those of Leon Battista Alberti, who may have been Piero's guarantor with Federico da Montefeltro, Lionello d'Este, and Malatesta [Longhi, Busignani]. Perhaps

the various visits and the work mentioned in sources from Ancona, Pesaro, and Bologna (*Catalogue* 34, 41, and 38) go back to the same period.

1452 Bicci di Lorenzo died. In 1447 the illustrious Aretine family of Bacci had commissioned him to decorate the choir of S. Francesco in Arezzo; Piero took his place and finished the work that had already been begun and which consisted of part of the ceiling (see **1459** and **1466**).

1454 4 October A stipulation in the contract ("in the painter's presence") with the Chapter of Sant'Agostino at Borgo San Sepolcro for the painting of the polyptych (*tabulam que est de tabulis compositam*) to place on the high altar of that church (*Catalogue* 23 A–H) within eight years (see **1469**). Directly afterwards the painter may have gone to Rome, where Vasari mentions that he paid a visit during the pontificate of Nicholas V (therefore before 24 March 1455, when the Pope died), and the remains of the frescoes in Sta Maria Maggiore must refer to this same visit [Longhi] (*Catalogue* 13).

1459 12 April Soon after he had finished the decoration of

Signatures and dates in paintings by Piero della Francesca: (above, on the left) *in* St Jerome and a Worshiper *in Venice (3),* (on the right) *in* St Jerome in Penitence *in Berlin (8), and* (underneath) *in* The Flagellation of Christ *in Urbino (11).*

S. Francesco in Arezzo (see **1452**), Piero was certainly in Rome. A document in the pontifical archives shows that he was paid 150 florins from the Pope's exchequer "for his share of the work on paintings [which] he carried out in His Holiness's bedroom." The paintings are confusingly mentioned by Vasari (see *Catalogue* 14). Pius II, another famous man in touch with Alberti, must have commissioned the work.

1460 The date MCCCCLX appears on the fresco depicting St Louis at Sansepolcro (*Catalogue* 18), under the Saint, but it is almost unanimously excluded from works known to be by him.

1462 Marco di Benedetto, brother of the painter, received from the Confraternity of the Misericordia of Borgo 15 scudi "in part payment of the picture which Pietro his brother has painted." One presumes that this payment was the balance due for the polyptych commissioned in 1445 (cf.) and judging by the words ("has painted") it had been recently finished [Longhi] in 1462. As for the employment of an assistant, one remembers that Piero was absent from Borgo, perhaps at Urbino or at Arezzo. In this period, between 1460 and 1465, Filarete [*Treatise on Architecture*], describing the ideal city of Sforzinda, mentions "Piero dal Borgho" as one among the greatest living artists capable of decorating it.

1465 On the evidence of a passage in the poem *De vita et morte illustris D. Baptistae Stortiae* by the humanist Ferabò of Verona [Cinquini, 1905] the diptych for the Duke and Duchess of Urbino

(*Catalogue* 22 A–D) must have been carried out in this year.

1466 20 December The Confraternity of the Annunciation of Arezzo commissioned Piero to paint a standard (lost) of the Annunciation (*Catalogue* 24). Those commissioning it state that he is the only artist capable of "carrying out the most beautiful possible work" after having "worked in Florence and here," referring to the great undertaking of the frescoes in S. Francesco. These therefore must have been finished (see **1452** and **1459**).

1467 While probably engaged in painting the banner in his native town, he carried out various public duties.

1468 He was at Bastia, near Sansepolcro, taking refuge from the plague "and in the said place he finished painting the said banner." [see **1466**]. At Bastia the work was received by Benedetto della Valle, treasurer of the Annunciation, and by two monks. Having paid Piero twenty-two gold florins "for the remainder of the commission" they conveyed it in a cart to Arezzo and the following Sunday the whole company of the Annunciation approved it, declaring it "beautiful."

1469 On 8 April the Confraternity of Corpus Domini of Urbino refunded to Giovanni Santi, father of Raphael, ten *bolognini* disbursed by him "for the expenses of master Piero of Borgo who came to see the *taula* (picture) in order to paint it." C. Ricci (1910)

Presumed portrait of Piero della Francesca in the woodcut published by Vasari in the second edition of his Lives *[1568]. It is similar to the painting reproduced above.*

supposes that the picture in question was that now in the Brera (*Catalogue* 29); but, seeing that it was to be carried out for the Confraternity of Corpus Domini, it seems more reasonable to think [A. Venturi; etc.] that it was for a polyptych of the Eucharist. The *predella* of this polyptych had been painted two years earlier by Paolo Uccello or by one of his pupils, although originally the monks had commissioned Justus of Ghent in 1474, but had not been satisfied. This was obviously after the negotiations with Piero had fallen through. On 14 November the monks of Sant'Agostino in Borgo San Sepolcro compensated Piero with money and land for the polyptych commissioned in 1454 (cf.).

1471 23 February He is mentioned as one of those behindhand in paying a municipal tax at Borgo San Sepolcro.

1473 He signs a power of attorney in favor of his brother: he was evidently in his home town, perhaps busy carrying out the frescoes in the Badia (see **1474**). There is a mention of Piero in a sonnet by Niccolò Testa Cilenio, written at Ferrara between 1470 and 1475.

1474 12 April He receives payment for the frescoes (lost) in the Badia at Borgo San Sepolcro (*Catalogue* 31). After this there is no mention of Piero in any document in Borgo until 1478. It is presumed that he was at Urbino painting *The Senigallia Madonna* and the altarpiece now in the Brera (*Catalogue* 27 and 29) and also to present to Duke Federico II his treatise on perspective: *De Prospectiva Pingendi* (see *Appendix*).

1475 From certain receipts relating to this year— moreover in accord with a fairly old tradition—it appears that Piero is the painter of a well-known fresco of 1475 in the Vatican showing Sixtus IV and the librarian Platina, sometimes attributed to Melozzo da Forlì. Although accepted by Zippel as by Piero [RDA 1919] the above-mentioned documents are considered to have been falsified [Longhi; etc.].

1478 The Confraternity of the Misericordia of Borgo San Sepolcro (see **1445**) commissioned a fresco of the Madonna which Piero was to carry out on a wall "between [their] Church and the Hospital"; there are no later references to this work (*Catalogue* 32).

1479 *The Resurrection* (*Catalogue* 19) is transferred from its original wall to the Town Hall of Borgo San Sepolcro where it now is [Procacci, in Tolnay, 1955].

1480 The municipality of Borgo San Sepolcro allocates money for the restoration of a wall "where Piero had painted *The Resurrection*" (*Catalogue* 19).

1480–82 During these two years he is head of the priors of the pious Confraternity of San Bartolomeo at Borgo San Sepolcro.

1482 22 April From the lady Giacosa, widow of Ganimede Borelli, he rents at Rimini a house with the use of garden and well. Perhaps he intended to make a long stay there. Local history makes no mention of it and therefore it probably came to nothing.

1487 5 July Piero *in extremo aetatis suae* but "sound in mind, intellect and body" instructs the notary, Lionardo of Ser Mario Fedeli, to draw up

Claimed as a portrait of PETRVS DE FRANCISCA/EX NOBILI FRANCISCOR[um] FAMILIA/PICTVRAE ARITMETICAE GEOMETRIAE/AMPLIFICATOR; canvas (178 × 118 cm.), which has come from Marini Franceschi's house at Sansepolcro to the city's Town Hall (46). The painting is usually attributed to Santi di Tito.

his will from notes jotted down by the painter himself on a sheet of paper, discovered by G. Mancini [AAL 1915]: "I desire to be buried in the Badia in our family grave. "I leave to the Badia vestry board ten lire. "I leave to the Body of Christ [Company of Corpus Domini] ten lire. "and to the Madonna of the Badia ten lire. "and ten lire to the Madonna of Reghia. "and from what remains half to

Antonio my brother and if Antonio dies before me to his male heirs and the other half to Marco's heirs, that is Francesco Bastiano and Girolamo and if one dies then everything to the other." The expression "sound . . . of body" seems to indicate that Piero was not blind as early biographers, following Vasari, have believed. In 1556, in old age, a certain Marco di Longaro, a maker of street lanterns, told Berto degli Alberti, who made a note of it, "that Marco, when a child, used to lead master Piero di la Francesca about, an excellent painter who had become blind: so he told me."

1492 12 October Book III of the Dead of the Company of San Benedetto at Borgo San Sepolcro (Sansepolcro, Town Museum) registers the death of "M. Piero di Benedetto de' Franceschi, famous painter, on 12 October 1492, buried in the Badia."

1509 Fra' Luca Pacioli publishes in Venice his treatise *De Divina Proportione*. It is considered plagiarism, a downright copy of *Libellus de Quinque Corporibus* composed by Piero della Francesca after 1482 and dedicated to Guidobaldo da Montefeltro (see *Appendix*).

Catalogue of works

An outline of the artistic formation and early activity of Piero della Francesca can be given only with caution from the moment when, in his first work, certain stylistic preferences appear already perfected. The only known fact in the chronology of his youthful activity is his presence in Florence with Domenico Veneziano, proved by a document (see *Outline Biography* and also for all future similar references) of 1439. Nevertheless, this document is open to two interpretations: that Piero arrived in Florence in the company of Domenico after having accompanied him on his Umbrian journey, or, on the contrary, that he had already been in the city for some years. In 1439 Piero must have been over twenty – perhaps over twenty-five; that is, he had reached an age when an artist's early formation can be considered finished. The profound knowledge of Florentine tradition and, in particular, of the science of perspective shown in Piero's early work, seems to suggest that he had made a prolonged stay in the city of the Medici prior to his collaboration with the Venetian master. Perhaps, as Clark suggests, he went to Florence after an early apprenticeship at Borgo San Sepolcro under a local painter such as Antonio d'Anghiari who in 1430 received the commission for the altar in S. Francesco, later given to Sassetta. This does not exclude the possibility of Piero's interest in Sienese tradition, of repeated journeys in the neighborhood of Arezzo to look at the polyptych in the parish church by Pietro Lorenzetti, and of ideas gathered from the work of Domenico di Bartolo, such as his *Madonna and Child*, now in the Pinacoteca of Siena, dated 1433. Toesca was the first to point out resemblances to Bartolo in Piero's early work. As for Sassetta's *St Francis*, Piero might have known it only after his return home from Florence; on the other hand, Longhi has clearly drawn attention to the Florentine influences apparent in Piero's work, reminiscent of Angelico. In any case Florence's rich cultural artistic

background between 1430 and 1440 is more than enough to explain the orientation of Piero's early work, whether in *The Polyptych of the Misericordia* or *The Baptism of Christ* (*Catalogue* 7 and 4).

If Piero were in Florence during 1439, and perhaps from 1435, both contemporary and past influences on him must be considered before Domenico Veneziano's arrival. Among the many names suggested, from Masaccio to Masolino, from Paolo Uccello to Angelico, from Donatello to Nanni di Banco, from Ghiberti to Michelozzo and Luca della Robbia or even the fourteenth-century Maso, certain artists can be ruled out as scarcely probable. Domenico Veneziano's letter from Perugia to Piero de' Medici in April 1438 mentions "fra Filippo and fra Giovane" as the artists supreme in the field of Florentine painting; and there is no reason to think that Domenico was wrong and ill-informed about artistic matters in Florence. It would be natural to suppose that a newcomer, such as Piero, would turn his attention to the work of artists of the highest repute, and of the two men mentioned in Veneziano's letter, Piero would have preferred Angelico, whose significance as an "interpreter of Masaccio's and Brunelleschi's ideas to the younger generation" was recognized by Longhi [1942]. Angelico's arrangement of space, the tranquil distribution of his figures, the firm composition and the luminous color of his work carried out between 1430 and 1440 must have appeared exemplary to Piero. He could not have found a master better able to prepare him for the solemnity of Masaccio's frescoes in the Carmine and the study of proportion in *The Trinity* in Sta Maria Novella. It is unnecessary to complicate the problem of Piero's early orientation, remembering that his preferences would be as immediate and as definite as the development of his style was sure and coherent. To these influences must be added what he learnt when working in collaboration with Domenico Veneziano who, having arrived

in Florence with his individual contribution as an "intimate" colorist and of painting "more free and rich in fine pictorial qualities," probably opened his young collaborator's eyes to the possibility of creating between figures and space a more "natural" relationship than the purely mathematical and quantitative one of Florentine tradition. His probable association with Alberti, too, must have given him that unshakable faith in the value of the laws of perspective and proportion – just at that time formulated by the architect in *Della Pittura* – which never left him. From the older parts of *The Polyptych of the Misericordia*, with their more robust, Masaccesque quality, to *The Baptism of Christ*, rich in mysterious harmony between the rustic figures and the vast luminous landscape, to the heraldic and ceremonial stiffness of the fresco in the Malatesta Temple at Rimini (10), it seems that Piero gradually developed his Florentine heritage, but moving intuitively with ever greater certainty and coherence towards the idea that there exists in nature a harmonious link between forms with each other and with space, and that this link gradually reveals itself in the pictorial microcosm in a unifying and tranquil vision, finding its law in the rationality of number and still more in "divine" proportion, based on an infallible structure of geometrical and quantitative relations, hidden, dissimulated, and continually transfigured in the infinite richness and variation of tones of light and color.

Piero's great chance of proving the richness of his vision – he had already given proof of it in the courts of Ferrara, Rimini, and Urbino – came when, on the death of the modest Bicci di Lorenzo, he accepted the task of carrying on the hardly begun cycle of frescoes on the story of the True Cross in the Gothic church of S. Francesco in Arezzo (15), a center a little apart from the prevailing cultural currents, but not far from Sansepolcro. Removed from the striving ambition and ostentation of court life it seems

that his native air was propitious to the artist. It favored his inclination to work out more fully the means to express his individual "naturalness," which made his painting as epic and serious as it was simple and fundamental. Thus, under his hand, the legend of the True Cross becomes a chapter in the history of Salvation: a spectacular story but never merely a profane chronicle; rather it is changed in every episode into the contemplation of an epic story yet to unfold, or already ended, from the beginning of time. If from Masaccio Piero learnt more profoundly than anyone else the art of ennobling the simplest daily events by the grandeur of his forms and the natural gravity of gestures which express the supreme and most conscious awareness of moral dignity, he does not neglect the accent on concentrated drama. Piero does not portray events or actions, but rather a contemplation of events, or a ritual repetition of actions and gestures which have existed from time immemorial. His characters are not protagonists, moved by passions and contradictions, caught up in the present, in what is going to happen, but impassive performers moving solemnly according to changeless ceremonial. Hence the sacramental character of his compositions even in battle scenes, even in the episode of the "judicial proceeding" of the torture of the Jew (15, F and I, and 15 G). A sacral character invests even the space itself in which Piero's figures stand, neither dominating nor dominated, but in serene proportional harmony, because created according to the same rational laws of measurement and the simplification of masses, governing all aspects of reality: an earthly paradise of nature, not yet aware of the fall of man or of his regeneration at the end of time. He presents man awakened at his first perfection, at the same time as the triumphant Christ of *The Resurrection* at Sansepolcro (19).

During the seventh and eighth decades of the century, relations were more frequent

with the Urbino court of the Montefeltro. It became at that time the center "of the intellectual art of the Renaissance, the art that is the most skillful game of artist-mathematicians" [Chastel]. But Piero's developing theoretical interests, far from being reduced to a "game," even if "most skillful," were to be expressed throughout his treatises: *De Prospectiva Pingendi* and *Libellus de Quinque Corporibus Regularibus*, written in order to show the possibility of making visible every aspect of reality according to a rigid mathematical order of the Creator. They seem at the same time to have increased his interest in certain stylistic and technical aspects of Flemish painting, specially in certain light effects (the Polyptych in Perugia and *The Senigallia Madonna* [25 and 27]). Light becomes a unifying element in the vision. In Piero's last works (*The Nativity* in London and *The Brera Altarpiece* [28 and 29]) the most balanced, monumental, rational structure coincides with the presentation, always more splendidly pictorial, that is tonal, of light [Longhi], and with the expression of an integral luminous universe, within which forms – men and things – purified of plastic definition, reveal themselves in their essence in perfect space, freed from any suggestion of time and incapable of any change.

Some remarks of a technical nature must be made. In the information at the head of each numbered paragraph in this *Catalogue*, the reader will often find the particulars relating to technique incomplete. In these cases – in the absence of specific details in the paragraph – it is almost certain that the artist used a combination of tempera and oil, probably learnt from Domenico Veneziano. In regard to frescoes, the use of cartoons (as well as *sinopia*) and of perforation, in order to transfer on to plaster, is most evident in Arezzo, and also in Rimini (10): for example, in the color plates XVII (at the bottom), XXII, and XXVII (in this last one can see the double perforation between the eye and the mouth of the

2 A

2 B

central figure, the outline of the ear in the figure on the left, and in the curve of the veil).

1 ⊞ ⊕ ⎯⎯ 1439 ⊟ ⦂

Frescoes, formerly in Florence, Church of Sant' Egidio (Choir)
These are the first known works by Piero (see *Outline Biography*), in which he assisted in illustrating the life of the Virgin, carried out under the direction of Domenico Veneziano, praised by Vasari and later destroyed.

2 ⊞ ⊕ 53×41 ⊟ ⦂
1440*?

A. MADONNA AND CHILD
Florence, Contini Bonacossi Collection
An inscription on the back records that the work, thought to be by Leonardo, was restored in 1655 by the Florentine painter Alessandro Rosi, whose repainting was removed in about 1940. Longhi [1942] attributed it to Piero, as the earliest of his known works, that is executed about 1440, during the time he worked with Domenico Veneziano. Longhi drew attention to the research in perspective shown in the two figures, in accordance with the Florentine tradition of those years, and also sketched on the back of the picture (see 2 B). Salmi [1947] accepts Longhi's opinion, but other critics hesitate without actually rejecting it. The cataloguers of the exhibition of "Four Painters of the Early Renaissance" (Florence, 1954) describe it as "attributed to Piero." Bianconi agrees; Clark is silent about it; Bottari declares that it could well be the work of the painter from Borgo. The surface appears somewhat worn.

B. VASE
On the back of the preceding picture. It is called a "study in perspective." Longhi sees in it the "perfect model" for the intarsia work

that Cristoforo da Lendinara was to carry out in the middle of the sixteenth century. In a bad state of preservation because of numerous missing parts.

3 ⊞ ⊕ 40×42 ⊟ ⦂
1448-50*

ST JEROME AND A WORSHIPER Venice, Accademia
On the tree trunk on the left, on which stands a crucifix, is written: PETRI DE BV[R]GO S[AN]C[T]I SEP/VLCRI OPVS; and on the right beneath the worshiper: HIER. AMADI. AVG. F. Cicogna [*Inscrizioni Veneziane*, VI, 1853] found in *Zibaldoni Morelliani* that Aglietti had seen this painting in Renier's house in Venice (through whom it reached the present gallery in 1850) and he traced various information about the Amadi family, St Jerome, and the probable worshiper, son of Agostino and Pellegrina Piscina, who may have lived in the middle of the fifteenth century. Soon after, Cavalcaselle [1864], studying the possibility of the worshiper being a member of the Amadi family – the Franceso who had commissioned in 1408 from Nicolo di Pietro a *Madonna* in the church of Sta Maria dei Miracoli in Venice, built by the Amadi, was a member of this family – but ended by rejecting the idea that *St Jerome* had been painted in Venice, because there was nothing Venetian in the landscape nor in the worshiper, and because he thought that the second inscription was false. This opinion had many consequences (see the catalogue of the above-mentioned Florentine review). Further, according to tradition, the landscape in the background is that of Sansepolcro. Berenson [1897] listed the picture as *St Jerome and Jerome Amadio*, but other critics have recognized in the worshiper a Malatesta. In spite of this, Longhi [1927] denied that the inscription was false (the opinion of recent Venetian gallery cataloguers [1955] is divided) and [1942] not only alleged that the inscription proved the picture to have been commissioned by a Venetian, but also saw in it a proof that Piero had paid a visit to Venice in about 1450 after his stay in Ferrara. Finally [1962] he rejected the idea that the background was of Sansepolcro, pointing out that it had exclusively Venetian charac-

3 (Plate XII)

teristics in the chimneys, like towers or chalices, rising from Venetian roofs. He dated the picture, as did Bottari, just before the middle of the century; Witting, on the contrary, thought it later; Ricci [1910] suggested 1453–4; A. Venturi [1911], having judged it to be contemporary with the frescoes at Arezzo, dated it 1465–6 [1922]; Clark and Bianconi think it belongs to 1450–5. As Longhi recognized, it shows the influence of Domenico Veneziano, specially in the

4 (Pls XIII–XVI)

landscape, like that in *The Baptism of Christ* (4), where in the landscape itself and in the lower parts of the worshiper, there are stylistic characteristics of Flemish origin, easily understandable after Piero's stay in Ferrara. But the formal relationship between the figures and the background is not convincing and it is thought that the picture may have been cut down to the detriment of its general harmony. Without a doubt it is chronologically near *The Baptism*: later than the two saints on the left in *The Polyptych of the Misericordia* (7, F and G) and perhaps contemporary with the two saints on the right (7, I and J); strangely enough it is reminiscent of Masaccio, while going back to Domenico Veneziano in the preponderance of the figures.

4 ⊞ ⊕ 167×116 ⊟ ⦂
1448-50*

THE BAPTISM OF CHRIST
London, National Gallery
There is no detailed information about the commission, but it was almost certainly painted for the Priory of S. Giovanni

Battista at Sansepolcro, from where – according to a considerably later record (Pichi [1835]), but reliable – it seems that it was removed to the city's cathedral in 1807 at the time of the suppression of the religious orders; then Sir J.C. Robinson bought it (1857) for 23,000 lire and handed it over to M. Uzielli. At the latter's London sale on 13 April 1861 it was acquired for the National Gallery. At the Priory in about 1465 two side panels and a *predella* were added, painted by Matteo di Giovanni, with the coats of arms of the Graziani family. While it is agreed that it is by Piero, the dates suggested range between 1440 and 1445 [Longhi] and 1465 [M. Logan, RA 1905], the latter based on a study of no validity of Matteo's side panels. Clark, followed by Bianconi and others, finds difficulty in dating it earlier than the saints on the left of *The Crucifixion* in *The Polyptych of the Misericordia* (7, F, G, and A), and puts it as late as 1450–5; but it seems unlikely that *The Baptism* was painted five years later than *St Jerome* in Venice, and the two year period 1448–50 seems more probable. This was a period when Piero was overcoming the influence of characteristics derived from Masaccio, visible in the early work for *The Misericordia Polyptych*, and returning to a freer rhythm, in the style of Domenico Veneziano. This style flowered in an organization of space much more complex and strict; an organization imposed on an absolute harmony of color and proportion between the figures and the background, where the human element, the action, the "story'

in fact, do not assert themselves and the air flows freely, creating depth in space, in spite of the intarsia effect of the various elements in the composition. Clark remarks on a resemblance between this landscape and *The Battle of Constantine* in Arezzo (15 F); but he is making a general comparison. This scholar subjects the composition to a geometrical analysis, dividing it into "compartments" in Alberti's manner, but it is difficult to admit that Piero followed this procedure; Clark also attaches a symbolic value to the youth to be baptized, suggesting that his limpid nudity symbolizes the freshness of the new religion, in contrast to the heavy military cloaks of the men in the background, and that the youth's head covered by his shirt symbolizes that baptism is the first step towards regeneration, etc. It is more important to notice with Davies [1961] that this same figure appears in *The Baptism* in S. Medardo di Arcevia, painted by Signorelli in 1508, and that it appears, in reverse, in the same subject painted by Nicolas Poussin, now in the National Gallery of Art in Washington [Camesasca, *Artisti in Bottega*, 1966]. Davies points out some "alterations," in particular to the feet of the angel on the left. There is a vertical split in the center of the picture, matching the join between the two parts of the wood; moreover the painting is heavily scratched and spoilt by serious peeling due to an old restorer. This has apparently been proved by the work of restoration in 1966, carried out in order to remove spurious painting at the sides of the curved part.

5 ⊞ ⊕ ⎯⎯ *1449* ⊟ ⦂

FRESCOES
Ferrara, formerly in the Estense Castle
Vasari mentions these frescoes saying that "Piero was invited to Ferrara by Duke Borso and in the palace there painted many rooms, afterwards destroyed by the old Duke Ercole so that he could modernize the palace." Salmi [RT 1943] thinks that the frescoes must have been earlier than 1450, because their stylistic characteristics are apparent in Ferrarese miniatures which he dates 1448; yet if one is to accept Vasari's statement in regard to the commission, they would have to be dated after 1 October 1450 when Borso succeeded Leonello on the ducal throne. It is thought that the frescoes were already destroyed by 1469; but one has to take into consideration that "old Ercole," that is Ercole I, succeeded Borso in August 1471. Moreover, together with the work in Sant'Agostino in the same city (see 6) they are mentioned – although as ruined – by Piacenza [in Vasari, edited by Bottari, II, 1771]. It is generally accepted, following Longhi and Salmi

himself, that these frescoes were important for the future development of painting and intarsia in Ferrara.

6  *1449*

FRESCOES
Ferrara, formerly in the Church of Sant'Agostino
Mentioned by Vasari at the same time as the preceding frescoes (which see for further details) as Piero's only surviving work in Ferrara. He mentions them as forming the decoration of a "chapel" suffering from the damp. It may be that Piacenza's remarks (see 5) regarding their precarious state of survival in the second half of the eighteenth century refer only to these latter frescoes.

The Polyptych of the Misericordia

The whole painting — made up of twenty-three pictures (273 × 323 cm. over all) — is in the Town Hall in Sansepolcro. It was commissioned from Piero on 11 February 1445 by the Confraternity of the Misericordia of Borgo San Sepolcro; the contract — published by Milanesi [B 1885] — stipulates that the altarpiece "*deauratam de auro fino et coloratam de finis coloribus, et maximis de azurro ultramarino*" (according to the usual contract making sure of the quality of the material) must be entirely by Piero's hand (not an unusual, yet not a usual, clause, in most cases depending on the price to be paid) and must be completed in three years. Moreover the artist undertook to inspect the work for ten years after it was finished and to make good any damage; such a precaution (this indeed unusual) was

added when the medium employed was a mixture of tempera and oil, a technique learnt by Piero from Domenico Veneziano. On the other hand, Cavalcaselle, followed by Longhi, discounts the use of tempera only, while Escher [1925] thinks it was painted only in tempera. A considerable part of the work was entrusted to assistants and went on for nearly fifteen years. A document of 1462 [Gronau RFK 1900] — which shows that a payment was made of "fifteen scudi in part payment of the painting by m. Pietro," to Marco di Benedetto, brother of the painter — seems to refer to the commission of 1445. The Confraternity, until its dissolution in 1807, owned the Polyptych; but already in the seventeenth century it had been broken up and its original framework had been replaced by a heavy, bulky, baroque construction. It was then moved to the church of S. Rocco and to its present position in 1901. Nine years before, and four hundred years after Piero's death, the Florentine G. Parrini arranged it in its present frame. After World War II it was restored under the supervision of the galleries of Florence.
Vasari [1550] recalls that Piero painted "in fresco" a Madonna della Misericordia for a pious congregation; early annotators of *Le Vite*, misunderstanding the allusion — evidently referring to another work now lost (see 32) — thought it referred to this Polyptych, and stated that it was all his own work [cf. Masselli, I, 1835]. Rosini [III, 1837], Passavant [*Raffaello...*, 1839], and G. F. Pichi [1892] gave further information about the Polyptych but always

attributed all the work to Piero. Already in 1864 Cavalcaselle pointed out that collaborators had worked on the "less important" parts, and attributed to another painter the complete responsibility for the *predella*, which he thought came from another work. Witting [1898], on this assumption, turned his attention to a careful study of Piero's assistants in a lively but not entirely convincing piece of criticism. Witting discovered in the *predella*, beside Piero's hand, that of Girolamo di Giovanni da Camerino, but this opinion was not accepted and was disproved by Weisbach [RFK 1899]. A. Venturi [1911] at first thought that Piero was responsible only for the five principal pictures, that the small paintings above were carried out by pupils working from sketches by the master, and that the saints at the sides and on the *predella* were of inferior workmanship; but later [1922] he became less definite and was hardly certain about even the *predella*. Möller van den Bruck thought it might be by Gentile da Fabriano but Graber [1920] ascribed it to Piero, and Giglioli [*Guida di San Sepolcro*, 1921] contested this and supported the opinion that the inexpert work of an assistant can be recognized in the "secondary" zones and particularly in the *predella*. Longhi [1927] excluded Piero from direct work on the *predella* and on the six small saints on the two outer pilasters. He assigned them to a different painter, probably a Florentine who worked in an individual manner or only vaguely tried to adapt his technique to the master's. It was Longhi who connected the Polyptych with the above-mentioned document of 1462

7 A (Plate I)

and put forward by way of confirmation the fact that among the figures painted by Piero is St Bernardino, who was only canonized in 1450. Moreover, because of evident stylistic discrepancies, this scholar suggested a chronological sequence spread over fifteen years: beginning with *St Sebastian* and *St John the Baptist* (7, F and G), it takes in the two large saints on the right (7, I and J) and the small paintings crowning the work (7, A, B, C, D, and E), and comes finally to the central panel (7 H). Van Marle [XI, 1929] dated the execution of the whole of the Polyptych after the Arezzo frescoes (15). Berenson [1932] considered the *predella* a spurious addition and Toesca welcomed Longhi's ideas, now the most widely accepted. Focillon, judging the whole painting an early work of Piero's, detected in the *predella* reminiscences of Angelico, so that he put forward the names of Baldovinetti or Giovanni di Francesco; but Salmi [1942] suggested, instead, the miniature painter Giuliano Amidei, and thought that he was also the painter of the saints on the side pilasters. Finally, Clark, sharing Salmi's opinion only in thinking that Piero's mysterious assistant was a miniature painter, made Longhi's proposed chronology more definite by assigning the central picture (7 H) to between 1449 and 1451 and dating later the two paintings of *The Annunciation* (7, C and D); in his opinion the *predella* was carried out (at least the two episodes on the right) from drawings by Piero, and Clark also sees Piero's hand in the Bishop Saint at the top of the side pilaster on the right (7 K).
For further details, particularly

on the chronology, see the following descriptions of the different parts. As they are limited to the work in which, by the consent of recent criticism, Piero's hand can be accepted, the paintings on the *predella*, where his hand is not recognized, must be mentioned here. They consist of seven pictures. At each end is an identical painting of the Confraternity's arms, then, from left to right, are *The Prayer in the Garden*, *The Flagellation*, *The Deposition in the Tomb*, *"Noli me tangere,"* and *The Maries at the Tomb*. As for the saints on the side pilasters, it is difficult to be sure of their identification.

7  81×52,5 1448*

A. THE CRUCIFIXION
It has several times been pointed out that there are similar color harmonies in the cuspidal panels painted by Masaccio on the same theme in the Polyptych in the Carmine Church in Pisa. The dramatic emphasis of movement by which the Madonna's grief is expressed seems in truth unusual in Piero's art; yet in comparison with the desperation or the emotional abandonment of Masaccio's figures, the gestures in Piero's picture — the Madonna's arms stretched out to the Son and the Evangelist's flung wide — are more solemn, almost liturgical, and devoid of emphasis; even the Christ appears more unmoved, without the writhing and prostration of the Pisan Christ. The gold background, transformed by Masaccio into a backcloth for the bas relief, acquires in Piero's painting an atmospheric value. *The Crucifixion* is universally acknowledged as Piero's. There are cracks and a few missing pieces.

The Polyptych of the Misericordia (7) as it appears today in the Art Gallery of Sansepolcro. The various parts, formerly covered by the original frame, have been mounted in unpolished wood.

7  54×21 *1455*

B. ST BENEDICT OF NORCIA

Although most recent scholars accept this as Piero's work, Clark discerns possible slight touches by the same assistant who painted the six saints on the pilasters. St Benedict is of the same date as St Andrew and St Bernardino in the principal tier. Spoilt by cracks and burns, specially on the background.

7  55×20,5 *1445*?

C. ANGEL OF THE ANNUNCIATION

Recognized as by Piero and as being of the same date as the preceding and as the other figures in the cuspidal frames (see, however, Clark's different opinion in the above introduction). State of preservation is the same as in *St Benedict* (7 B). It is worth noticing that *The Angel of the Annunciation* and *St Francis* (7, D and E) are in different states of preservation, although resembling each other, so that one speculates as to whether they could have been painted at different times or whether their subsequent history was different.

7  54×21 *1445*?

D. THE VIRGIN ANNUNCIATE

The attribution and chronology are the same as for the preceding. As in *St Francis* (7 E), it is covered with a thick network of cracks rather deeper than in the other two cuspidal paintings (see also 7 C).

7  54,5×21 *1455*

E. ST FRANCIS OF ASSISI

The authorship and chronology

7 F (Plate IV)

7 G (Plate IV)

7 I (Plate V)

7 J (Plate V)

are the same as for 7 B; as regards the state of preservation, see 7 C.

7  108×45 1445-48

F. ST SEBASTIAN

Unanimously considered as Piero's work and the first picture of the Polyptych to be painted. The figure, drawn with energy and an almost rough plasticism, clearly recalls Florentine painting especially that of Masaccio, in the firm articulation of the limbs and the definite contrasts between light and shade. Piero's masterly capacity in his mature work of placing the most characteristic features in harmony and perfect proportional relationship with the rest of his composition is not yet apparent. The painting suffers from numerous scratches and a few cracks.

7  108×45 1445-48

G. ST JOHN THE BAPTIST

As regards authorship, date, and state of preservation, see 7 F. Florentine elements are particularly evident in the firm characterization of the face and in the swelling movement of the drapery.

7 134×91 *1460*?

H. THE MADONNA OF THE MISERICORDIA

The tradition that the foreshortened worshiper with head thrown back is a self-portrait goes back a long way [Coleschi, *History of San Sepolcro*, 1886]; in fact the worshiper has some resemblance to the engraving in Vasari's *Vite* (see page 84) and with the sleeping soldier in

The Resurrection (19), also supposed to be a self-portrait. Del Vita [RA 1920] goes further and suggests that all the worshipers are portraits of Piero's relatives. Few critics have accepted either suggestion. Longhi denies both. Clark leans doubtfully to the first. Ricci [1910] sees a resemblance between the worshiper in profile, the supposed Amadi in *St Jerome* in Venice (3), and one of the spectators in *The Battle between Heraclius and Chosroes* at Arezzo (15 I). It may be accepted as Piero's work, but suggestions in regard to date differ widely: Longhi perceives greater maturity than in the other parts of the Polyptych and thinks that the heads of the worshipers approach the "complex pictorial experience which dominates in Uffizi Diptych [1465–6; n. 22]"; Focillon sees in the worshipers strong links with Masaccio's

intense characterization; Clark, without giving any reasons, dates the picture just before or just after Piero's journeys to Ferrara and Rimini (1449 or 1451) and discerns in the Madonna's pose similarity with that of the *St Francis* (now in the Berenson Collection at Settignano) painted by Sassetta for the same Confraternity of the Misericordia of San Borgo in 1444. Bianconi perceives similarity between the worshipers and the two figures in *The Crucifixion* (7 A) but does not suggest any date for either picture, and other critics are even more vague. One can see that the gesture of the worshiper in the foreground seems to repeat with less violence that of the Evangelist in *The Crucifixion* above, and the woman kneeling beside him raises his clasped hands in a gesture that echoes that of the sorrowing Madonna; but Piero tended to repeat, with greater or less variation, the same poses. In these two worshipers the drapery towards the bottom has a movement "à la Flamande," yet the folds, like organ pipes, are to be found in many frescoes in Arezzo; in particular, the worshiper seen from the back has shoulders similar to those of the man in the foreground on the left in *The Meeting of Solomon and the Queen of Sheeba* (15 B); and in this *Meeting* and in *The Discovery of the Cross* (15 H) faces – defined with intensity but without insistence on the features – alternate between front view, three-quarters view, quarter view, and profile. Finally, and what is most important, circular space is created and defined by the spread of the mantle and the position of the worshipers: one can speak of a true recess with absolute certainty and conviction; and, within it, the figures assume an impassivity in perfect consonance with the true and genuine "framework" of the Virgin's figure. It seems reasonable to agree with Longhi that this picture was

7 B (Plate II)

7 C (Plate II)

7 D (Plate III)

7 E (Plate III)

the last one painted for the Polyptych and carried out in about 1460.

I. ST ANDREW
Piero's authorship is certain and it is generally admitted that the figure of the apostle (and *St Bernardino*, 7 J) was painted some years after the two saints on the left (7, F and G). In simplifying the drapery, which has lost the metallic sharpness of the Baptist's mantle, there is a calmer and more sure arrangement of space in relation, too, with the overall economy of the Polyptych, and a less emphatic type of feature. State of preservation similar to that of 7 F.

7 ⊞ ⊕ 109×45 1455* ▤ ⦂

J. ST BERNARDINO OF SIENA
It is unanimously agreed that it is by Piero, and Longhi's chronology is coming to be accepted in regard to the spreading of St Bernardino's cult beyond Siena not much earlier than ten years after his canonization in 1450. State of preservation similar to the foregoing.

7 ⊞ ⊕ 41×18,5 1460*? ▤ ⦂

K. BISHOP SAINT
The only one of the small figures on the pilasters which must be mentioned, because of Clark's opinion that it was painted by Piero. It is difficult to admit this without also including the figure underneath and the one next to it on the left; it seems more reasonable to accept – developing Longhi's view – that these figures are the most successful among those which an unknown artist tried to paint in the style of Piero.

8 ⊞ ⊕ 51×38 1450? ▤ ⦂

ST JEROME IN PENITENCE
Berlin, Staatliche Museen
In the course of cleaning the inscription PETRI DE BVRGO OPVS MCCCCL (see below) has appeared on a scroll at the bottom on the right. Bode [JPK] recognized the painting as by Piero only in 1924. Scholars have agreed, except Toesca, who declares it "very unconvincing." Berenson, including it in his *Indici* of 1932, ascribed only the figure of the saint to Piero: and Longhi, who had not examined it in 1927, confined [1942] the limits of Piero's authorship to the design and composition of a few zones (as well as the saint, the stool for books, the rock with the niche, the inkstand and, on the left, the unfinished lion, the path, "a few sprigs of the distant trees," and the narrow area of light in

7 H (Pls VI–VII)

7 K

the background) and the work must have been repainted with an unsure touch and finished at the end of the fifteenth century by another artist (to whom must be due the middle distance, the taller trees, the sky, and details of the background). Finally [1962] Longhi expressed doubts about the genuineness of the date on the scroll, giving as his reason the impossibility of dating the painting earlier than *St Jerome* in Venice (3), and thought it was painted during Piero's period of activity with Domenico Veneziano, that is soon after 1440.

9 ⊞ ⊕ 44,5×34,5 1451? ▤ ⦂

PORTRAIT OF SIGIS-MONDO PANDOLFO MALATESTA
Florence, Contini Bonacossi Collection
It came here about 1930 from

the D'Ancona Collection of Milan, and was brought there from St Petersburg in 1889. Morelli recognized it as Piero's work [cf. Morelli's correspondence with Richter, published in Baden Baden, 1960], but modern critics do not accept it as Piero's; only Longhi [1942] attributed it to the master. It was shown in the exhibition of "Four Painters of the early Renaissance" [Florence, 1954] as "attributed to Piero." Not even Bianconi accepted this, while Clark did not mention it. According to Longhi it served as a model for the painting at Rimini (10), and indeed the head is of the same dimensions as in the fresco. A work of high quality, in which simplified masses are skillfully suggested by light and achieve the proud, firm plasticity of sculpture.

ST SIGISMUND AND SIGISMONDO PANDOLFO MALATESTA
Rimini, Tempio Malatestiano
On the frame at the bottom is the inscription: SANCTVS SIGISMVNDVS PANDVL-FVS MALATESTA. PAN. F. PETRI DE BVRGO OPVS MCCCCLI. On the circular frame of a castle on the right one reads: CASTELLVM SISMVNDVM ARIMIN-ENSE MCCCCXLVI; and this last date (1446) – clearly relating to the Malatesta fortress (the building in the picture) – was given to the painting by Marcheselli [*Pictures of the Churches of Rimini*, 1754], followed by Oretti [ms. Municipal Library of Bologna, c. 1765], by Lanzi and by Sighinolfi [RC 1913]; Dennistoun, interpreting it in the same way, read it as 1445. Battaglini [in *Basinii . . . works*, 1794] and Zani [*Enciclopedia . . . IX*, id.] had correctly attributed to the fresco the date at the bottom; and Ricci [*Tempio Malatestiano*, 1925] confirmed it, as it referred to the date of dedication of the chapel where the picture stood. We therefore possess one of the rare definite dates in Piero's chronology. The last two letters "LI" are no longer legible, but they were visible up to 1794 when the composition was engraved by Rosaspina [in Battaglini]. All scholars attribute the fresco to Piero except Rosini [*Storia . . III*, 1837], who thought it might be by Signorelli. As Longhi says [1942], the background between the pillars has been transformed from a flawless piece of marble into a "space open to the sky" during a seventeenth-century restoration. Against this background kneels the Lord of Rimini in the attitude of paying homage to his patron saint, King of Burgundy; and on the right, two greyhounds, in attitude and

color like armorial supporters, complete the diagonal which, beginning with the figure on the throne, defines the profundity of the space. Above the two dogs the castle appears far off through a circular window and must not be taken for a medallion in low relief. Both Malatesta's profile and the view of Rocca were compared with a well-known medallion by Matteo de' Pasti; but the comparison is very vague; the fortress, although taken from the same point of view as in the medal, is not the same; and the profile is quite different from the one drawn by Pasti. It resembles in style the frescoes in Arezzo, where King Solomon's head (15 B) shows a close resemblance to that of St Sigismund. One may agree

8 (Plate XI)

9

SANCTVS SIGISMVNDVS · SIGISMVNDVS PANDVLEVS MALATESTA PAN . .

10 (Plate XVII)

12   13

with L. Venturi that the arrangement of the patron saint and the worshiper is reminiscent of *St Jerome* in Venice (3) but the spatial and rhythmic articulation is incomparably firmer, achieving a greater detachment, liturgical rather than ceremonial in its effect. In regard to the setting, Clark stresses the influence of Alberti and this is Piero's only fresco which appears to be subordinated to the architecture into which it is fitted. The work, very much damaged, was badly restored by the Capizucchi in 1820; about 1950 the overpainting was removed and the fresco was transferred to canvas.

11 〔symbols〕 59×81,5 1455*

THE FLAGELLATION OF CHRIST
Urbino, National Gallery of the Marches

On the base of the throne on the left is the inscription: OPVS PETRI DE BVRGO S[AN]C[T]I SEPVLCR[I]. On the right, underneath the three figures in the foreground, in 1839 Passavant [*Raffaello . . .*, 1882–91] read *"convenerunt in unum"*, taken from the second verse of the second Psalm referring to the Passion of Christ (*"Adstiterunt reges terrae, et principes convenerunt in unum adversus Dominum et adversus Christum eius"*) and used in the service for Good Friday, a verse which often appears in illuminated manuscripts illustrating the Flagellation, as Clark has pointed out. Ever since 1700 close study of the subject of the painting has caused controversy among scholars. As efforts to identify the men on the right, specially the last two, by comparing them with figures on medallions and other evidence, have produced no definite results, we give the principal suggestions. According to tradition, the fair young man (in the group on the right) is Oddantonio da Montefeltro; and on each side are his ministers, the evil counsellors Manfredo dei

Pio and Tommaso dell'Agnello, responsible for the popular indignation and conspiracy of the Serafini which caused the death of the young prince (1444), half-brother of Federico da Montefeltro. Thus the painting was thought to commemorate Oddantonio's end. Another early idea: the three figures are lords of Urbino, predecessors of Federico. Pichi [1892], understanding the inscription which has disappeared as *"convenerunt in eum"*, suggested Oddantonio and the leaders of his principal enemies Serafini and Ricciarelli. For Clark *The Flagellation* symbolizes the tribulations of the Church, culminating in the fall of Constantinople (1453); the bearded man being a learned Greek, inspired by the Emperor Paleologus; and the picture could refer to the Council of Mantua (1459) or to a council subsequent to the tragic event: nor, in truth, is this view contradicted, but rather borne out, by the inscription *"convenerunt in unum"*. Clark's objections to the traditional interpretations seem convincing: the three figures do not look like, respectively, a tyrant (or a prince – moreover the young man is barefoot) and two wicked counsellors, and there is no reason why his successor should have commemorated the murder, and still less have associated it with the Passion of Christ. The suggestion that the subject depicts a "moral Flagellation" carried out by the two ministers is even less tenable.

The painting was exhibited in its present position in the nineteenth century and in 1861 Cavalcaselle and Morelli [GNI] valued it surprisingly at 15,000 lire, whereas, Longhi states, they valued *The Martyrdom of St Sebastian* by Baroccio [in the same Gallery] at 30,000 lire. Before that it was in the old sacristy in the Cathedral of Urbino; while there it was mentioned by Father P.G. Vernacchia in an eighteenth-century manuscript:

"The flagellation of Our Lord Jesus Christ, with the figures and portraits of the Dukes Guidobaldo and Oddo d'Antonio [sic]." M.A. Dolci [ms. formerly belonging to Pungileoni (*Elogio . . . di G. Santi*, 1822)] records it as being in the cathedral in 1775 and upheld Piero's authorship against that of Mantegna (it is unknown who suggested the latter). After Pungileoni, Piero's authorship was unanimously accepted. But opinions in regard to its date vary: according to Rosini [*Storia . . .*, III, 1837], it was one of his first works; for Cavalcaselle [1864] and Berenson [1911] about 1469 (at the same time as Piero's stay in Urbino, for which there is proof); late according to Witting; between 1465 and 1466 in the opinion of Ricci [1910] and A. Venturi [1911]; while Longhi [1927] followed by Van Marle [1929] and Salmi [1945] dated it shortly after 1444 (in accordance with the traditional interpretation of the subject) and before the Rimini fresco (10) and those of Arezzo (15); then Toesca again insisted on 1460 as a limit *ante quem non*; Clark anticipated this by a little (1455–60), followed by Ragghianti [in Baldini, 1954], L. Venturi, and Bianconi. Longhi himself, who in 1942 agreed with the preceding opinion,

dated it earlier [1962], but in any case before the Arezzo cycle, and this has been accepted by Bottari (1444–51) and by Busignani. Clark based his ideas on the date both on his esoteric interpretation of the work and because "it is inconceivable that Piero could have invented this architectural style without the example of Alberti, and at that time [c. 1445] Alberti was only beginning to turn his attention to the subject." This scholar proposes a complex analysis of the proportions of the composition: the scale is given by the strip of black marble inlay above the head of the bearded figure on the right, and this "unity" constitutes the tenth part of the width of the picture and the seventh part of the height; the central column is four units high and half a unit wide and its displacement from the central axis of the composition is half a unit to the right. The affinities that Clark points out with the Arezzo cycle seem more convincing: the head of the bearded man resembles Constantine's in *The Battle* (15 F) and the architectural plan recalls the background of *The Meeting of Solomon and the Queen of Sheba* (15 B); but in *The Flagellation* the welding between the two zones is more immediate, more severely balanced, and at once suggests the relationship between "event and memory" [Formaggi] or, rather, the link in contemplation between the figures in the foreground and the torture of Christ. Clark's iconology succeeds, therefore, in convincing and, as for his "reading" of formal values, one must accept what he says in regard to the relationships in space of the golden section between the two "areas" (his "reading" was the starting point for Wittkower and Carter's later analysis [JWCI 1953] which came to the conclusion that the work is constructed on two different scales; one relating to the "open" space on the right; the other to where the torture scene takes place; further, the comprehensive plan including the arrangement of the figures and of every smallest part, depends on precise elements of "symbolical mathematics." One cannot ignore Longhi's opinion that

"even in the sense of almost exalted mathematical demonstration in the structure of the whole picture, when compared with the general artistic developments of the fifteenth century, reveals the beginning of the parabola of Piero's genius"; nor deny the resemblance he points out between the angels in *The Baptism* (4) in London and the so-called Oddantonio. The examination by Rome's Central Institute of Restoration (c. 1950) showed that the painting has several damaged parts (paint has flaked off and there are two horizontal cracks) concealed, at least partially, by old repainting which deadens the incredible luminosity.

12 〔symbols〕 130×105 1455-60

ST JULIAN (?)
Sansepolcro, Municipal Museum

The saint's identification, claimed by Salmi [BA 1955] was generally accepted, but not by Bianconi. The fresco came to light on 23 December 1954 in the apse of the old church of Sant'Agostino, which was reconsecrated – (see page 100) – to St Clare. Notice of the find was given by R. Papini [CDS 1955] and by Salmi [cit.]; the attribution proposed by the two scholars was unanimously accepted. As regards chronology, opinions differ from 1475 [Papini]; 1460–65 [Bianconi; Bottari]; and earlier than 1460 [Longhi, 1962]. As the saint resembles the prophet on the right in the Arezzo cycle in S. Francesco (15 N), Longhi's opinion, if it allows one to date the picture as far back as 1455, is the most reliable. In proof of Piero's knowledge of ancient Roman paintings assumed by Berenson [CDS 1961], Camesasca [*Artisti in bottega*, 1966] compares the head with that of a young hero discovered in the *triclinium* of a villa at Castellamare di Stabia.

13 〔symbols〕 1459?

ST LUKE, EVANGELIST
Rome, Church of Sta Maria Maggiore

This is what remains visible of the pictorial decoration in the chapel of St Michael and St

11 (Plate VIII–X)

Peter ad Vincula in the above-mentioned church. According to Vasari the decoration was carried out by Benozzo Gozzoli, and Biasiotti [BA 1913] also attributed it to him; but at the same time Galassi [A 1913] attributed it to Piero's Roman school and soon decided that it was by a follower showing affinities with Lorenzo da Viterbo [Lavagnino — Moschini, *The Churches of Rome*, no date]. It was Longhi himself [1927] who attributed it to Piero and dated it 1459 or 1455 (see *Outline Biography*) because "the style is that of the second series of frescoes at Arezzo"; there must therefore have been an interruption in the work on the Arezzo cycle during Piero's first journey to Rome in 1455 which is mentioned by Vasari. Most scholars agree; and recently Busignano added his confirmation, noting in St Luke "a close connection" between *The Meeting of Solomon and the Queen of Sheba* and *The Battle at the Milvian Bridge* (15, B and F). Clark, however, has doubts and thinks that the fresco may have been painted by an assistant from Piero's design. The evangelist's head is like that of the officer in *The Torture of the Jew* (15 G) which is thought to be by a pupil of Piero's; but the painting's bad state of preservation (spoilt by discoloration and extensive disappearance of the paint) gives a poor impression of its quality.

14

Frescoes, formerly in Rome, the Vatican (Stanza di Eliodoro [?])

A document in the papal Archives [*Introitus et Exitus*], of 12 April 1459, records the payment of a hundred and fifty florins to Piero "for his share of the work on paintings [which] he carried out in his Holiness's bedroom." Zippel [RA 1919], who published the document, accepted as genuine certain receipts with the date 1475 which Mancini [in Vasari, 1917] said were false, and Longhi declared were forged "with the object of corroborating the mistaken tradition attributing to Piero the fresco by Melozzo [da Forlì] for Sixtus IV's library." Taking into consideration the date, 1459, the "work" must refer to the pontificate of Pius II. Vasari, on the other hand, in his biography of Piero, states that the master "being invited to Rome by Pope Nicolas V, painted two scenes in the upper chambers of the palace . . . which were destroyed by Pope Julius II in order that Raphael of Urbino might paint the Imprisonment of Peter and the Miracle of the Corporal at Bolsena," so this means that the work must have been begun before 24 March 1455, when Nicolas V died (see 13). But Vasari may have become confused; in the biography of Raphael he writes of only one episode painted by Piero.

The Frescoes in San Francesco of Arezzo

The mural cycle, dedicated to the legendary stories of the True Cross, decorates the walls of the choir in the church of S. Francesco in Arezzo. Baccio di Magio, a chemist of Arezzo, in his will of 6 August 1416 made provision for a window in the chapel of S. Francesco, of which he was patron, and for the walls to be decorated by Niccolo Tedesco; the testator died the following year. A document of 1427 shows that Francesco, son of Baccio, had put aside a sum of money for the pictorial decoration of the choir in this same church [Mancini, in Vasari, 1917]. From a book of commemoration belonging to Francesco Bacci one learns that this same Francesco with his nephews, Andrea di Tommaso and Agnolo di Gerolamo, entrusted the work to the Florentine Bicci di Lorenzo. He set to work on the vault and the underside of the choir arch. On his death (1452) the work was unfinished; *The Last Judgment* had been painted on the entrance wall, the four *Evangelists* on the vault (together with minor decoration) and two *Doctors of the Church* on the inside of the arch [Salmi, RDA 1916]. It is generally accepted that Piero had already taken over the work in 1452, that is, it seems clear that after Bicci's death the work was not interrupted for long. Stylistic considerations show that Piero's fresco at Rimini (10) dated 1451 and the first frescoed stories in Arezzo are closely linked. Bicci had taken part in the decoration of Sant'Egidio in Florence, under the direction of Domenico Veneziano, for whom Piero also was working, and this must have been one among many reasons why those commissioning the frescoes at Arezzo chose the painter from Borgo.

No proofs exist to show whether the choice of subject was imposed by the Bacci (with or without recourse to specialists in similar "programs") or suggested by Bicci di Lorenzo or by Piero. As mentioned above, the incidents in the legend of the Cross of Christ, as set forth by the Genoese Bishop Jacopo da Varazze (or Voragine), the literary source for various similar cycles, were most popular in the Middle Ages, particularly in Franciscan churches. According to Clark, this popularity in the middle of the century can be explained by the fact that men's minds turned to these legends in response to the events of the time, brought home by the pressure of the Turks and the coming to an end of the Byzantine Empire in the East. This is an extremely interesting idea, especially when one re-

members that during Piero's stay in Florence that city was the seat of council for numerous prelates, doctors, and important men from Byzantium; but one must also remember that not much time had elapsed since Cenni di Francesco had depicted stories of the Cross in the Franciscan church near Volterra. Piero accepted (or found already established) the traditional system of a wall divided horizontally into three tiers of which the two rectangles "approximated to the golden section" [Longhi, P 1950]. This arrangement was due to the necessity for creating symmetrical harmony and not in order that the artist's illustrations for the stories should follow a strictly chronological order. The episodes at the top of the lateral walls fit into the lunettes, and the parallelism between *The Death of Adam* and *The Exaltation of the Cross* (15, A and J) painted there seems intentional. Each episode, and what is beneath (this is less obvious on the lower level), is divided into two parts — as in *The Flagellation*, in Urbino (11) — by a vertical element, usually slightly to the right of center, which has the value of a caesura. On the lateral walls, too, episodes taking place in the open air face each other, as do the two most courtly and ceremonial pictures (15, B and H) on the second tier and the two battles (F and I) below. Moreover on the back wall the two prophets (M and N) on each side of the window balance each other; the middle spaces below the prophets are occupied by two more "popular" incidents (C and G) and on the bottom row are the most solemn (D and E). This analysis goes back to Graber [1920] and has often been quoted and elaborated; but in the effort towards a clear "external" symmetry, made more evident by not linking together the various episodes by perspective (each has been drawn from a separate view point) it remains to observe with Clark the search for contrasts in the planning of the various zones: contrasts of color and light. Longhi [id.] drew attention to the fact that the theme limits the master to a certain extent, in spite of his gift of transforming the "long and adventurous poetic romance built round the sacred story," giving it the broad sweep of a profane and secular epic, and a ceremonial, formal liturgical note. The artist succeeded in giving new life and actuality to a picturesque medieval legend, at once fantastic, popular, and edifying, and creating a serious, most solemn "sacred play." As always with Piero, the accent does not fall on the action of the story, but he presents the facts and people caught up in time, made eternal, motionless, due to his search for absolute perfection of form and the full harmony between proportion and spatial elements. Antal's thesis [*Florentine Painting . . .* 1947] that the famous cycle

celebrates the *Weltanschauung* of the bourgeoisie, that is to say the views of those who commissioned the cycle, was rightly denied by scholars [Longhi, 1963; etc.]. For Muratov [*Immagini d'Italia* (in Russian), 1925], every composition in the series concerns the destiny of the whole human race, and for Alpatov [CM 1963] these "stories" are expressions of the phases through which human beings pass (from patriarchal simplicity [see 15 J] to life in a "modern" city and in courts [15, H and B], to the glory of empire with its invincible regular army [15, I and F], and the exaltation of nature, purified from what is extraneous, fortuitous, and superfluous. Thus to insist on the "extended spectacle of appearances," on the rendering of the macrocosm as an "eternal and obvious spectacle," could mean on the one hand divesting Piero's work of its rich cultural

references and on the other of its evocative power. One is bound to agree with Longhi that Piero did not achieve a perfect unity between conception and execution because of the Gothic ambiance in which he worked.

As mentioned above, Piero's work began in 1452; 1459 is usually given as the date of its completion (the year in which the master's presence in Rome is known from documents concerning his work in the Vatican); it is nevertheless possible that work on the cycle went on beyond the sixth decade, even to 1466 (see *Outline Biography*). Some observations by Longhi on the internal chronology of the series are particularly interesting: *The Annunciation* (15 D) could have been painted before *The Meeting* (15 B) because "a few traces of Tuscan linear decoration complicate certain parts of the work"; *The Discovery* (15 H) could precede *The*

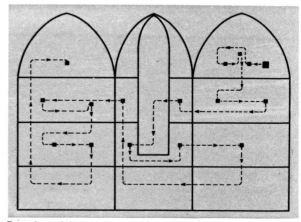

Two plans of the mural cycle of Arezzo (15). In the upper one are letters — of the zones connected with Piero's work — that refer to the descriptive sections in the present Catalogue. *The lower plan shows the historic sequence of the illustrated episodes (small black squares indicate the order and the large black one the beginning) followed in the* Catalogue *itself.*

Meeting; The Exaltation (15 J) could have been painted at the same time as the earlier episodes on the "evidence of decoration in the borders which has a Florentine flavor." As for the rest, the order followed would coincide with the usual practice: it would follow the successive removals of the scaffolding from top to bottom. Clark gives good reason to believe that the part on the right (west wall) was done first, before Piero went to Rome; after the Roman interlude another five years were spent carrying out, with great help from assistants, the left (east) wall. Clark notices a difference in tonality between the two walls; that of the west wall painted first is more luminous — that is much cooler — but more transparent; the colors of the east wall being warmer and less clear. The arrangement of the scaffolding, therefore, may have been different and the cycle painted in vertical sections and not in horizontal zones.

The frescoes, forgotten for

15 A (Plate XIX)

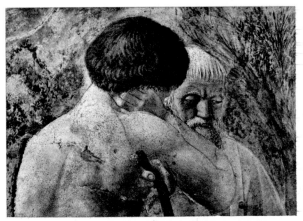

Details from 15 A [Pl. XIX] (above). The head of the fourth figure from the left, before recent restoration: one can discern old retouching and the flaking off of color produced by humidity. (Below) busts of onlookers (fourth and third figures from the right) in their present condition: the branches in the background painted on dry plaster have almost disappeared. The back of the young man shows damage caused by humidity.

centuries, were much damaged, particularly because the walls, standing on their own, were bound with metal girders, and the clamps — apart from the jolting and other misfortunes which befall old mural paintings — caused extensive damage. Restoration (perhaps following several other partial restorations) was carried out in 1858 by G. Bianchi. His numerous efforts at the comprehensive restoration of missing parts caused critics to believe that the copies carried out twenty years later by the Frenchman Loyeux (now in the chapel of the École des Beaux-Arts in Paris) gave a true impression of the original cycle; but perhaps the watercolors by the German Ramboux, painted between 1816 and 1842 (now in the Düsseldorf Academy) give a truer impression. A later effort at restoration (1915) by D. Fiscali won Longhi's approval in that it "definitely" strengthened the walls and removed the iron clamps disfiguring the center of the episodes and moved them to the outer ornamental framework. Clark doubts the efficacy of this work, alleging that there has been a diminution in the colors. Bianconi suggested that this was caused by dust rising from the brick floor. Fiscali, having removed Bianchi's arbitrary additions, treated the gaps left with a "harmonious color wash" — as it was called — which, instead of standing out from the original, aimed at "merging" with it. From 1959 until 1965 a new effort was made, directed by L. Tintori for the Galleries of Florence. The man responsible for the new "campaign" recognized that after Fiscali's work no further considerable deterioration in the colors had taken place; the color, instead, seemed to be spoilt by raised patches, not in evidence before 1915, but now increasing (so

much so as to form "craters" of unstable material) and visible in old photographs. The causes of the phenomenon were discovered: they were due in part to the accumulation of dust (specially from the floor) and more particularly to humidity. Water infiltrated through the roof and worked on the fixatives used by previous restorers, causing them to contract and to become oxidized. Here was the reason for the numerous microscopic flakings of the paint and the general lowering of the color tones. It was widespread because the process was affecting, although in different ways, the whole cycle and becoming evident even in the best preserved areas, as in The Meeting (15 B). Having removed the detritus from the ceilings (thus eliminating the chief source of humidity), and the old fixatives which, as they deteriorated, had flecked the frescoes with gray, and the raised additions caused by restoration, Tintori set to work to repair the frescoes and lower the level of humidity by means of a synthetic resin, very resistant to the action of water, paraloid B 72 (later eliminated from the surfaces in order to avoid alteration). The conclusion of the work (to be considered as provisional because treatment has yet to be decided for widespread damage that has come to light) aroused misgivings which have given rise to heated controversy in newspapers [see in particular CDS 1965] and on television. According to the well-known restorer M. Pellicioli, and Longhi himself, Tintori has committed two fundamental errors: a too drastic cleaning with the consequent loss of the original light color washes (the cycle appears more cold and crude than in the past), and the choice of fixative (that employed would irremediably

spoil the preservation of the frescoes). Tintori supports his work by saying that he has removed only the spurious additions (some were in tempera, others in pastel and still others in pencil — these last confined to shading or "renewing" of shadows and parts of the landscape — all, according to him, very easy to distinguish from the original painting): as to the fixative, described by him as absolutely transparent, he has quoted the chemical experiments (carried out under the superintendence of the Council of Fine Arts in the Institute of Fine Arts at the University of New York and the Mellon Institute of Pittsburgh) proving that it cannot alter for fifty years (while the lacquergum suggested by Pellicioli, apart from being subject to glaze, would become irremovable). In any case, Tintori [VA 1963] has expressed the fears that remain in regard to the preservation of the foundation of the whole cycle, that is the actual plaster. This is being undermined by a phenomenon (unexplained in origin) in which new upheavals of color (with renewed formation of "craters" and the scaling mentioned above) may only be prevented by transferring the frescoes onto a new background. To help the reader understand the incidents represented, the detailed description of individual parts of the cycle does not follow the order of their position (in any case easy to reconstruct from the plans on page 91), nor the order in which they were painted (not definitely known, as has been pointed out) but the narrative of The Golden Legend from which are taken numerous quotations from the story. After the various episodes concerning the Cross, the last parts of the cycle, attributed to Piero by modern scholars, will be discussed.

15 B (Pls XX–XXVII)

(Above) *women's heads (second and third to the right) in* The Adoration of the Sacred Wood *(15 B) before recent restoration: the heaving up of the paint found in many areas shows damage caused by humidity and other causes.* (Below, right) *other details of the same group of women: showing the blurred effect brought about by dust and the chemical change in old fixatives* (left); *and after recent cleaning, carried out over the whole surface except in the darkest part at the bottom in the center* (to the right).

15 ▦ ✠ 390×747 1452* ▤ ⁝

A. THE DEATH OF ADAM
On the right, Adam, having reached the age of nine hundred and thirty years, and being near death (he is sitting on the ground and Eve supports his head) asks his son Seth (the fair-haired man between the youth leaning on a stick and the woman front face) to go to the angel "at the gates of the earthly Paradise" to obtain the "oil of mercy"; directly on the left, in the background, the

archangel Michael refuses Seth the oil of salvation and instead gives him some seeds from the tree of Sin to place in the mouth of the Patriarch, who will die three days later, and when they "bear fruit" his father will be "cured and whole"; on the left is the burial of Adam, under whose tongue Seth had placed the "little seeds"; in fact "planted that small twig" which "when planted grew into a great tree", the tree dominating the center of the composition "and it

lasted until the time of Solomon." On the left of the fresco dramatic emotions are portrayed such as are not found in the rest of the cycle; in particular the woman in front of the tree, raising her arms and repeating with greater emphasis the gesture of St John in *The Crucifixion* of *The Polyptych of the Misericordia* (7 A); and the prominence given to the drama is heightened by comparison with the grave solemnity of the scene on the right. Both Longhi and Clark refer to affinities with archaic Greek statuary; the former points out certain derivations in this fresco, recognizable not only in Signorelli, but also (as regards Eve's head) in the Cumean Sibyl, painted by Michelangelo on the ceiling of the Sistine Chapel in Rome. This fresco, according to Longhi, is entirely Piero's work; Clark thinks that the two youths on the extreme left are by an unknown assistant. It is spoilt by extensive missing portions as well as minor damage.

15 ▦ ✠ 336×747 1452* ▤ ⁝

B. THE ADORATION OF THE SACRED WOOD and **THE MEETING OF SOLOMON AND THE QUEEN OF SHEBA**
Having flourished until the reign of Solomon (see 15 A) the tree that had arisen from Adam's tomb was cut down by the king's order, but the wood cut from it was no use, being always too large or too small, so that "the craftsmen, exasperated, rejected it and threw it down where it could serve as a bridge for wayfarers" over a small lake ("a little stream of running water") called Siloam. The Queen of Sheba, having arrived to "hear Solomon's wisdom and wishing to cross the water where the plank had been placed, saw in a vision that the Saviour of the world would be fastened [suspended, crucified] on this piece of wood and, therefore, did not wish to cross over on it"; she knelt down to worship it, as one sees on the left, surrounded by her ladies, while,

on the extreme left, in front of the two large trees in the background, her grooms wait with the horses. On the right, between "a line of Corinthian columns divinely measured" [Vasari] Solomon with his dignitaries welcomes the Queen and her ladies. In the text of *The Golden Legend* the Queen's reception is given no particular prominence; the importance given it by Piero reveals his interest in courtly society, for the dignified rhythm of ceremonial rather than for display. Alpatov [1963] makes the importance given to the present episode depend on an esoteric "program" (see the introduction to the cycle); he stresses Piero's minimal concern with differentiating the characters: the Queen of Sheba wears a crown, but only in the picture on the left, not in the other, and she is differently dressed in the two parts of the fresco; while Solomon's face resembles Chosroes's in the painting (15 I). The composition of the two episodes recalls *The Flagellation* at Urbino (11) so

15 C

15 D (Pls XXVIII–XXIX)

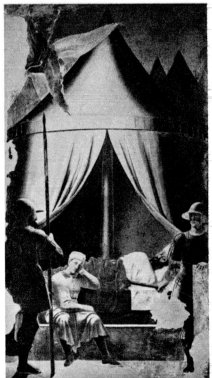

15 E (Plate XXXII)

15 G (Pls XXX–XXXI)

clearly that one critic has talked of a composition in reverse. This would not be surprising in Piero who, according to another custom (whose purpose has been shown as being anything but an easy expedient [see 7 and 17]), seems to have used with few variants a single cartoon in two parts for the group of women in *The Adoration* and in *The Meeting*. The composition is considered one of the most carefully worked out. The architectural elements and those of the landscape achieve an equal value in the spatial arrangement; and the figures too, due to the synthesis between faces and drapery, have

a fine "architectonic" character. In regard to the drapery one remembers Vasari's description: "Piero was in the habit of making clay models, covering them with soft cloth with a number of folds in order to copy them and turn them to account." Nevertheless, the artist does not neglect the portrayal of his own fantasy in conformity with the laws of perspective: Nicco Fasola notes that his low view point gives a "paradoxical" stature to the figures in the foreground "but even the figures in the hall have a certain independence within the architectural structure; and it suffices to notice the different levels of the

capitals"; thus the group of people gathered between the columns is freely arranged against the surrounding architecture "to heighten the human interest." Scholars agree that Piero was helped by assistants, especially with the painting of the grooms on the left. The name of Giovanni da Piamonte is suggested both for this painting and for others. There are three large areas of damage.

15 ⊞ ⊕ 356×190 *1455*? 目⋮

C. THE CARRYING OF THE SACRED WOOD
Solomon, having learnt from the Queen of Sheba that "on

that wood" forming the little bridge "would be crucified One for whose death the kingdom of the Jews would be destroyed," has it removed so that it may be buried "in the profoundest depths of the earth." However, sometimes the picture is understood as illustrating the placing of the bridge ordered by Solomon himself: Alpatov [1963] notes that in fact the true theme is the exaltation of human labor. The ascent to Calvary is also suggested: the veining of the wood forms a kind of halo behind the bearer's head and his curling hair is reminiscent of the crown of thorns and the composition is typical of that of Christ carrying the Cross. The veining, according to Focillon, shows Piero's passionate attention to the inner meaning of things and reveals him as a "painter of reality." Bianconi points out that the graining of the wood corresponds to the "formal design traced by the clouds" in a composition based with great daring on a display of crossed diagonals and that it anticipates the design of *The Exaltation* (15 J) [Longhi]. Scholars agree that Piero received considerable help from assistants. Schmarsow [*Melozzo*, 1885] and Witting suggest Melozzo da Forlì after 1460; Longhi, followed by various modern scholars, suggests Giovanni da Piamonte because of numerous possible similarities in the altarpiece at Città di Castello, signed by him in 1456.

15 ⊞ ⊕ 329×193 *1455*? 目⋮

D. THE ANNUNCIATION
There have been many suggestions as to the interpretation of the theme. Springer [1880] thought that the fresco symbolized the announcement to the Empress Helena of the finding of the True Cross; but the iconography is typical of the Annunciation to Mary. According to Longhi the subject alludes to the Passion of Christ, which – in Clark's opinion – would appear out of place in this "courtly epic." The episode does not occur in *The Golden Legend*, which goes straight from the story of Solomon to that of Constantine. An effort has been made to find a link between the two stories, such as the Good Friday hymn to the Cross, where the reference to the Annunciation appears clear. Salmi, on the other hand, interpreting the subject as the announcement of death to the Madonna, traces a connection between the Old and the New Testament in the announcement of the life and death of Christ. In any case, there is an evident relationship, even in theme, between this *Annunciation* and *The Dream of Constantine* (15 E) on the opposite side of the window on the same level; both illustrate an angelic visitation. In the courtly solemnity of the composition are found a strictly geometrical framework and a spatial and proportional

harmony between the figures and the architecture (some scholars are reminded of the Ducal Palace in Urbino). According to Clark, the fresco, stylistically, is outside the sequence of the cycle and must have been painted in 1466. Except for Venturi [1911], who thought it was the work of an assistant, Piero's authorship is accepted. Large areas are missing and there are cracks and abrasions.

15 ⊞ ⊕ 329×190 *1455* 目⋮

E. THE DREAM OF CONSTANTINE
On the eve of the decisive battle against his rival Maxentius, Constantine was struck by fear of his enemy's imposing strength. During the night "he was awakened by an angel and commanded by him to look upwards"; obeying, he saw in the sky "the shape of the Holy Cross formed of the brightest light, and above it was written in letters of gold: 'In this sign shalt thou conquer.'" Above the tent in which the emperor sleeps, watched by two soldiers and an attendant, against the background of the tops of other tents is the holy messenger, almost in the shape of half a cross. The symmetry, similar to that in *The Annunciation*, and the distribution of the figures is made clear by the pole supporting the tent, corresponding in the other episode to the column, with the usual function of dividing the picture into two zones. Attention is drawn to the startling nocturnal light effects, often attributed to northern influences, in particular to the *Livre du cuer d'amour épris* by King René, datable with certainty to 1457. According to Longhi and most other scholars, the work is by Piero. Only Clark, though with doubts, thinks it could be by an assistant, perhaps Giovanni da Piamonte. Apart from several missing patches, there is serious damage, especially to the figure of the angel. A drawing (now in the British Museum, London) mentioned by Ottley [*The Italian Schools*

15 .F (Pls XXXIII–XXXV)

of Design, 1823, p. 58] as by Giorgione, which Cavalcaselle compares with this fresco and which later was ascribed by Witting to the School of Parma is thought by Longhi [1927] to be a late derivation.

15 ⊞ ⊕ 322×764 1458*? ▤ ⦂

F. THE BATTLE BETWEEN CONSTANTINE AND MAXENTIUS

Constantine "made joyous and sure now of victory" by his nocturnal vision (15 E) "displays before him the sign of the cross that he had seen in the sky and transforms the standard of war [that is, the battle standards] into signs of the Cross. He carries in his right hand a cross of gold" (which – unless the gold has come off and this is unlikely – Piero painted white [Pl. XXXV B]). He then implored God that his hand, thus "armed with the sign of salvation" should not be stained with the blood of Romans gathered in bands in his adversary's army; and Maxentius fell into the trap laid for him by Constantine at the Milvian Bridge and "was drowned in the deep river," which one sees on the right of the "caesura," formed by the landscape with the Tiber as seen at Sansepolcro: "that indescribable interlude of sunlit countryside, observed with the anxious and loving eye of the peasant who, concealing himself in a furrow, sees his peaceful life jeopar-

dized by the battle of Anghiari; he is familiar with the tree, the little house on the Tiber bridge, the shade under the mulberry tree, its branches reflected in the water" [Longhi, 1927]. As for the zone on the right, it must be completed by Vasari's description, which is less open to suspicion than Ramboux's copies, of having wrongly ignored the damaged parts of the fresco: ". . . where is the flight and submersion of Maxentius [painted by Piero] and a group of horses in foreshortening most marvelously executed which can be described as of surpassing excellence for those days. In the same scene he represented a man half-clothed and half-naked like a Saracen, riding bareback, very remarkable for anatomy, a thing little known then." Warburg [AC, 1912], judging from Ramboux's copies which he published, thought that Piero had given Constantine (in the center of the fresco, to the left of the landscape interlude) the appearance of the Byzantine Emperor, John Paleologus, taken from Pisanello's well-known medallion (1439); but Clark, pointing out the differences in the shape and rhythm of the two heads, thinks that Piero based his drawing rather on personal memories of Paleologus, whom he had presumably seen in Florence at the time of the council of 1439. In general composition one must compare the calm, solemn,

almost processional advance of the conquering army (dominated by the forest of raised lances "right up to the edge of the picture," similar to those which were to be raised "two centuries later in an immortal painting by Velasquez" [Longhi]), with the disorganized flight of Maxentius's troops; yet without the break between the two zones to be seen in his Death of Adam. Clark and others suggest the possibility of comparison with Paolo Uccello, whose gift of reducing shapes to fundamentals may have impressed Piero when on a visit to Florence before he went to Rome. It is agreed that Piero is responsible for the whole fresco, unfortunately the most damaged of the series.

15 ⊞ ⊕ 356×193 *1455*? ▤ ⦂

G. THE TORTURE OF THE JEW

Helena, Constantine's mother, summoned the Jews so that she might find out where Christ was crucified; a certain man called Judas was pointed out to her as the only man who knew the exact place; but he refused to reveal it. "She commanded that he should be thrown into a dry well and there tortured by hunger"; after six days of torment "on the seventh he begged to be raised and said that he would reveal the True Cross." The moment depicted in the fresco is when the Jew is being hauled up

from the well; and Longhi stresses the significance that "once again" Piero "has chosen to represent in the great legendary cycle a visual fragment or, rather, he has transformed a dramatic event into a pictorial scene." The concept of the composition, with the pyramid formed by the beams and the building on the left, appears strictly one of solid masses, especially the battlemented wall in the background which cuts off the composition and makes the enclosed space, measured with such care, more concrete. Scholars agree that assistants worked on the fresco. Clark thinks that their part in it was considerable and Longhi suggests the hand of Giovanni da Piamonte. There is extensive damage due to flaking of paint and cracks as well as discoloration.

15 ⊞ ⊕ 356×747 1460*? ▤ ⦂

H. THE DISCOVERY OF THE THREE CROSSES and THE PROVING OF THE TRUE CROSS

The outline of these episodes is given in The Golden Legend as follows: in the place pointed out by Judas an aroma of spices came forth so that the Jew was converted and rejoiced "openly" in the discovery. Having dug to a depth of "twenty paces" the hidden crosses come to light and are presented to St Helena. The left side of the fresco shows in

a single episode the finding and the presentation to the empress. The sovereign, with her retinue (including a dwarf), watch the work of digging. Vasari especially admired the figure in the middle section (" a workman leaning on a spade awaiting the commands of St Helena while the three crosses are being dug up, all of which cannot be improved"); in the background is Jerusalem with characteristics of Arezzo, dominated by the red façade of S. Francesco. There is some open country with vines, the slope of a hill, and then the firmly outlined shape of the church (that is the Temple of Venus, near which – according to The Golden Legend – were found the three crosses from Calvary); hence the second episode. "And, not being able to recognize the Cross of Christ from those of the two thieves, she (Queen Helena) had them brought to the center of the city where they awaited the glory of the Lord and at about the hour of noon a dead youth was brought for burial and Judas held up the bier and placed the first and then the second cross on the dead man's head, but nothing befell; then he held the third cross over him: immediately the dead man came to life." This is the incident shown in the fresco. The young man sits up, his body appearing vigorous in the morning light, while Helena, on her knees, worships the same wood as the Queen of Sheba

(Above) copy of the watercolor of 15 F painted about 1835–40 by A. Ramboux (Düsseldorf, Staatliche Kunstakademie): one notices the half-naked horseman towards the right fully described by Vasari. (On the right) fresco 15 F before recent restoration: in spite of extensive gaps there still remain many parts arbitrarily filled in by Bianchi and, perhaps, by earlier restorers.

15 H (Pls XXXVI–XLIII)

15 I (Pls XLIV–XLVIII)

in the fresco (15 B), surrounded by her ladies and watched by three men in strange oriental hats. As in *The Meeting*, the architectural elements assume definite importance in the composition, though here less strictly articulated, freer, and more varied. According to Longhi [P 1950] the architecture of the little temple is in the style of Alberti which reached Venice soon after, at about the same time as Piero's painting. There is no dramatic emphasis: everything takes place as in a solemn evocation of events fixed in immemorial time; a spectacle, which is the celebration of a rite. It is accepted that Piero carried out much of the work. Perhaps the hand of assistants can be recognized in the group round St Helena and the kneeling women on the right [Toesca]. As well as extensive

gaps (in the central part, towards the right and on both sides) there are many cracks, abrasions with flaking of color, and oxidization almost everywhere.

15 🎞 ⊕ 329 × 747 1460* 📋 ⁝

I. THE BATTLE BETWEEN HERACLIUS AND CHOSROES

In the year 615, according to *The Golden Legend*, the Persian King Chosroes had stolen the True Cross and had it encased in his throne, so that when sitting on it, like Almighty God, he had on his right the wood of the Cross instead of the Son and a cock on his left in place of the Holy Spirit – the cock is seen on the extreme right at the side of the faldstool under a canopy (pierced, strangely enough, in one part but not all over).

The Emperor Heraclius attacked the troops of the Persian King, defeating them "on the banks of the river Danube," as represented in three quarters of the fresco, beginning on the left. Having gained the victory, Heraclius proposed that Chosroes should become a Christian, but "not wishing to do so Heraclius drew out his dagger and cut off his head." This incident is taking place on the right in front of the throne. Among the people grouped round the defeated king who, on his knees and motionless, awaits his end, Vasari states that there are portraits of contemporaries ("Luigi Bacci . . . together with Charles and his other brothers," – perhaps to be identified with Francesco di Baccio and his nephews Andrea and Agnolo – "and of many Aretines, distinguished men of letters of the day.")

Such statements cannot be proved and many others have to be rejected as when, describing the affray, Vasari writes of "fear, animosity, skill, and force and all other emotions produced in a fight, as well as the accidents, with a great heap of wounded, of the fallen, and the dead." Focillon draws attention to the fact that the combatants "move without haste, like good workmen conscientiously intent on their profession of killing." Modern criticism recognizes that assistants must have helped in painting the fresco. Longhi attributes work to Lorentino d'Arezzo. The suggestion that Piero painted the fresco after his return from Rome is justified by the presence of classical traits; Warburg [AC 1912] notes, for example, an affinity between the warrior on a white horse in the foreground and a similar

group in a carving on the Arch of Constantine (15 H).

15 🎞 ⊕ 390 × 747 1460*? 📋 ⁝

J. THE EXALTATION OF THE CROSS

After the victory over Chosroes, Heraclius took the Cross with great pomp back to Jerusalem, but, just as he was entering the city, "the stones forming the entrance fell down," welding themselves together "like a wall"; an angel reminded him with what humility Christ had crossed this threshold seated on an ass. "Then the emperor, his face bathed in tears, took off his shoes and all his clothes except his shirt and taking the Lord's Cross bore it in humility to the gate"; as is shown in the fresco where – in spite of a missing central portion – Heraclius is seen barefoot, clad in white (but not in his shirt

15 J (Pls IL–LI)

only), while he offers the sacred wood to be worshiped by a group of kneeling citizens of Jerusalem, dominated by a figure in the act of doffing an enormous hat. In Heraclius's renunciation of imperial splendor Alpatov sees a theme balancing that in the lunette opposite (15 A) and a return

sistants worked on the fresco which, in Clark's opinion, is their work alone, carried out in Piero's absence in his workshop from his drawings. Modern criticism suggests no particular artist, but Schmarsow [*Melozzo*, 1885] and Witting attributed it to Melozzo da Forlì. Apart from the already-

mentioned damage there are many abrasions and some discoloration.

15 base cm. 55* 1452*

K. ANGEL'S HEAD
Carried out in order to complete the decoration of the vault, begun by Bicci di Lorenzo. Today critics admit that Piero della Francesca had some hand in it.

15 base cm. 55* 1452*

L. ANGEL'S HEAD
The same comment as for the previous fresco. There are doubts as to whether the drawing was by the master, although recent critics accept it as by him.

15 base cm. 193 1452*?

M. A PROPHET
It has been suggested that this figure and the one balancing

it on the other side are the prophets Jeremiah and Jonah, or perhaps St John the Evangelist who, in their writings, refer to the tree of the Cross; but one cannot be certain because of the lack of determining attributes. This prophet reminds one of St John, but not as Piero depicts him in *The Crucifixion* of Sansepolcro (7 A). Because of the obvious inferiority of the other prophet in the fresco, most recent critics attribute most of the work to an assistant, whom Longhi identifies as the same painter of "less important" parts in *The Polyptych of the Misericordia* (7), while Clark — and Bianconi — lean to Giovanni da Piamonte (see also 15 N). Bianconi thinks the work belongs to the second phase of the Arezzo frescoes, begun soon after 1460; other modern critics, agreeing with Longhi, think it was painted when Piero began the cycle.

15 K

15 L

to the simplicity of patriarchal days, solemnized – according to Alpatov – in *The Death of Adam*. As usual the composition is divided into two parts by a definite central "caesura" between two trees, where the Cross is the most important vertical element, corresponding – in the opposite lunette (15 A) – to the tree flourishing on Adam's tomb, with the obvious allusion to the symbolism between the first man's sin and Christ's work of redemption (". . . and wherever the Enemy had wrought harm He brought the cure"). Pératé [in *Histoire de l'Art* by A. Michel, 1908] points out that the composition achieves the "maximum effect by extreme simplification" and yet not beyond the limit "where it would have given the impression of poverty." All scholars agree that many as-

15 M

15 N (Plate LII)

15 base cm. 190 1452*?

N. A PROPHET
For the identification see 15 M. While Schmarsow [*Melozzo*, 1885] and Witting thought that both prophets came from the studio of Melozzo da Forlì, modern critics recognize Piero's hand. In his conception of the figure he reveals himself in one of his most discriminating moments; he chose a stance of grandiose immobility which "*ipso facto* changes into moral certainty" [Bianconi]. Contrary to general opinion which places it amongst Piero's early work in S. Francesco, Clark thinks it was painted only a little before 1459. In good condition except for the discoloration of the blue of the tunic.

15 base cm. 72 1452*

O. ST AUGUSTINE
With St Ambrose (15 P) it completes the series of the four Doctors of the Church

15 O

begun by Bicci di Lorenzo. The connection with Piero della Francesca is confirmed by the "coarseness that relates it to *The Baptist* of Sansepolcro" [7 G], pointed out by Longhi who, at the same time, draws attention to the refined quality of the color.

15 base cm. 72 1452*

P. ST AMBROSE
The same comments as for 15 O.

15 base cm. 70* 1460*

Q. CUPID
For its symbolic significance, see 15 T, bearing in mind that an exact interpretation is difficult today because the frescoes have disappeared in the upper part of the pedestal opposite

the entrance arch. Even modern scholars do not accept it as Piero's work or do not offer an opinion because of its poor state of preservation. But after the most recent work of restoration on the cycle it is evident that Piero had some hand in it, even if it is the work of an assistant.

15 ⊞ ⊕ base cm. 70*
1460* ▤ ⋮

R. ST LOUIS
It is agreed that it should be attributed to an assistant of Piero's whom Longhi identifies as Lorentino d'Arezzo.

15 ⊞ ⊕ base cm. 70*
1460* ▤ ⋮

S. ST PETER MARTYR
Longhi rightly considered it one of Piero's last works in this cycle because "the magnificently cubic masses of the head are obtained by contrasts in tone." Originally this was probably a full length figure.

15 ⊞ ⊕ base cm. 70*
1460* ▤ ⋮

T. AN ANGEL
It may personify divine love, in contrast to the cupid on the opposite pedestal (15 Q) [Alpatov, 1963]. It is unanimously attributed to Piero.

15 Q

15 S

15 T

16 (Plate LIII)

Longhi rightly considers that it was one of the cycle's later paintings; Clark, on the other hand, pointing out similarities with the central figure in the group in the foreground of *The Flagellation* at Urbino (11), thinks that it was an early work in this cycle. Originally a full length figure.

16 ⊞ ⊕ 190×180
1460 ▤ ⋮

ST MARY MAGDALEN
It is near the sacristy door where Vasari remembered seeing it. Unanimously attributed to Piero and contemporary with the last frescoes in S. Francesco in the same city: indeed, the tendency to model "almost directly by tones" pointed out by Longhi persuades one to associate it with *St Peter Martyr* of the Arezzo cycle (15 S). Clark explains that the powerful architectonic structure is a return, particularly as regards the drapery, to Florentine "sculptural" tradition (reminiscent of Masaccio and Donatello) which indeed Piero preferred for single static figures. Recent restoration carried out by L. Tintori for the Galleries of Florence has removed dirt and spurious additions; parts are missing and there are scratches and other damage, due above all to the fresco's position just above floor level.

17 ⊞ ⊕ 260×203
1460? ▤ ⋮

MADONNA DEL PARTO
Monterchi (Arezzo), Cemetery Chapel
The theme is unusual in Italian painting, though common in that of Spain. The Virgin of Hope points symbolically to the Child in her womb [Clark]; however, in a relief by Bartolomeo Buon, datable c. 1450 (Victoria and Albert Museum, London) the two themes of the Misericordia Madonna and the Virgin of Hope are united. The painting must have been ideal for the apse of the little chapel, but it was removed in 1911. From 1919 until 1925, after being restored, it was in the Municipal Art Gallery in Sansepolcro; then it returned to its original position where it is so much venerated by pregnant women that the Mayor of Monterchi dared not risk lending it for display in Florence in 1954, fearing possible reactions if, during its absence, a woman had a miscarriage. It is generally attributed to Piero, but Berenson [1897] attributed the design to Lorentino d'Arezzo, as did A. Venturi [1911]. In Piero's work the shapes are outlined less sharply than in this painting, but the hand of assistants only shows in secondary parts. Longhi's chronology is usually accepted; that is, 1450–5, at the same time as the first Arezzo frescoes. Clark – who states that this Madonna is even more "oriental" than the one painted for the Confraternity of the Misericordia (7 H) and reminds him of "early Chinese painting" – dates it about 1460, after Piero's journey to Rome. He associates it with the death of Piero's mother, who came from Monterchi and was probably buried there ("having finished his work in Rome [Piero della Francesca] returned to Borgo, his mother

17 (Plate XVIII)

painting, though common in that of Spain. The Virgin of having died . . ." [Vasari]): this would make it contemporary with the second series of Arezzo frescoes. The two angels pulling back the curtains of the pavilion are taken from the same cartoon in reverse: this repetition is not the result of any lack of imagination but – as in other work by Piero – it adds to the solemn, ceremonial tone with which he displays the Madonna's motionless, superb dignity, in spite of the pose, with the left hand on her hip and the right pointing to her womb. Mary's halo, in spite of serious damage, shows shining reflections, as depicted by Piero in other paintings (7, F, G, I, and J, etc.). Here the little floor tiles, which the perspective and composition hardly allow to be seen, are reflected. Apart from missing parts and considerable discoloration of the picture has been spoilt by the reconstruction of the upper part of the pavilion; it should be a reconstruction and not an effort at arbitrary integration.

18 ⊞ ⊕ 123×90
1460 ▤ ⋮

ST LOUIS
Sansepolcro, Municipal Art Gallery
Dragomanni [in Vasari, 1835] informs us that underneath the painting was the inscription: TEMPORE NOBILIS ET GENEROSI VIRI LODOVICI ACCIAIOLI PRO MAGNIFICO ET ECCELSO POPVLO FLORENTINO RECTORIS AC PRIMI VEXELLIFERI IVXTITIAE AERE BVRGIANO MCCCCLX, evidence of devotion and homage to his

patron saint from Acciaioli, appointed by the city of Florence governor of Borgo. The fresco remained in the Palazzo Pretorio of Sansepolcro until after 1850. It was attributed to Piero by Lanzi [AZK 1856], Cavalcaselle, G.F. Pichi, Berenson [1897], Witting, Waters, Gronau, Escher [HK 1922], and A. Venturi [1922], who had earlier attributed it to an assistant. Longhi, judging it to be rather poor, attributed it to Lorentino d'Arezzo, as did Van Marle, while Toesca thought it to be by an assistant working from a cartoon by Piero. Baldini and Bianconi do not attribute it to Piero. Clark thinks that Piero was directly associated with it. It is not in good condition; and was restored about 1950 by G. Rosi for the Galleries of Florence.

19 ⊞ ⊕ 225×200
1463-65 ▤ ⋮

THE RESURRECTION OF CHRIST
Sansepolcro, Municipal Art Gallery
Tradition suggests that the guardian painted full face, similar to a worshiper in *The Madonna of the Misericordia* (see 7 H), is a likeness of Piero. In the presentation one recognizes complex symbolical meanings. Clark remarks that the Risen Christ seems part of a dream weighing heavily on the sleeping soldiers; Tolnay [GBA 1954] points out that in fact only two of the men are asleep (perhaps dreaming the incident taking place behind them), the other two appear struck by the vision, and one is covering his eyes; so it is evident that the Risen Christ is to

be understood as the protector of Borgo, a vigilant sentinel over the sleeping city. Tolnay also suggests that deeper meanings should be perceived, and Clark that there is a link between the risen Christ and a rustic divinity. Gombrich opposed this opinion [BM 1952] asserting that it is contrary to fifteenth-century ideas. Tolnay insists on a cosmic theme and points out that the trees on the left are dry and leafless, whereas those on the right are green; this could be an allusion therefore to spring's eternal renewal, that is a direct link between the rebirth of nature and the Resurrection of Christ; the latter being the symbol of the former. Vasari mentions the fresco in his biography of Piero: "it is considered to be the best of all his works in that city [Sansepolcro]." In 1700 it was covered with whitewash and was unknown to Lanzi, but Rosini [III, 1839] knew it and ascribed it to Signorelli. It seems that originally it was not where it is now in the Palazzo Comunale (then the Palazzo dei Conservatori and now the Municipal Art Gallery), but was removed in 1480, or perhaps in 1474, according to a document to which Berti drew Tolnay's attention; and one can take it that on that occasion the Corinthian columns framing the picture were damaged or altered (perhaps when displayed in religious ceremonies) and that only the inner sides of the original picture remain. It is accepted as Piero's work, carried out at the same time as the last episodes on the east wall in S. Francesco at Arezzo, that is c. 1460. This seems reliable, although Tolnay has suggested a date after 1470. Nicco Fasola, analyzing the perspective plan of the fresco,

tried to ascertain its two view points, one of which "is at the height of the edge of the sarcophagus. . . . But the resurrected Christ does not belong entirely to this world and for this reason his naked torso and head are seen from such a low point of vision. Perhaps in drawing Christ Piero hesitated between the magnetic attraction of his expression and the strong purposeful action of the foot which is liberating the whole body from the tomb." There is a sense of suspension, of timeless immobility, intensified by the landscape, which is simplified although drenched in light.

20 ⊞ ⊕ 42×21 *1465 ▤ ⋮

MADONNA AND CHILD WITH FOUR ANGELS
Williamstown (Massachusetts), Clark Art Institute

Gnoli [D] published it only in 1930, when an American collector who "did not mean others to enjoy it" bought it from the art dealer Knoedler in Paris; therefore – except for the reproduction made available by Gnoli himself – it was impossible to study it until its recent arrival in its present position. This has given rise to doubts about its authenticity. Longhi [1942] dispelled these by making a careful analysis of the painting and declaring it a *"chef d'oeuvre."* He thinks that it was "destined for a court," this being shown by the "regal" interpretation of the theme. The relationship between the figures and the architecture is particularly carefully planned, though not solved with the sureness and feeling for space in Piero's other works: the column and the capital behind the Madonna's head, for ex-

19 (Plate LIX)

ample, lack the usual proportions and the composition is exceptionally crowded (not to mention the "bridge" between the figures and the onlooker formed by the angel on the right which is unique in Piero). The date of 1470 put forward by Gnoli is accepted by Busignani, but Longhi dates it between 1460–5 and not between 1465 (the date accepted by Bottari) and the end of that

21 ⊞ ⊕ 151×126 *1465* ▤ ⋮

HERCULES
Boston, Isabella Stewart Gardner Museum

It was painted in a house in Borgo San Sepolcro, perhaps belonging to Piero himself, and may have formed part of a series of "illustrious men." The choice of a pagan theme is unique in any known work by

sixteenth century a Graziani, and the house with the fresco belonged to that family, and then to the Collacchioni, one of whose members had the picture removed in 1860–70 to a villa he owned [Graziani, *l'Arte a Città di Castello*, 1897]; in 1896 it was taken back to its original place [Graber]; was acquired by the Florentine Volpi in 1903 and by the Gardner Collection three

20

18

decade. Further, although it has nothing in common with the frescoes in S. Francesco in Arezzo (if anything, the festoons decorating the mirrors in the background recall those in *St Sigismund* at Rimini [10]), the feeling of confined space recalls parts of the Perugia *Polyptych* (especially 25 A).

him. E. Franceschi Marini [CCE 1902] thought it had a connection with the legend, according to which Hercules liberated Monterchi, birthplace of Piero's mother, from a dragon. In regard to "external" evidence, a descendant of Marco, brother of the painter, called Isolante, married in the

21

years later. From the time that Graziani published a reproduction it has been accepted as Piero's work and Longhi [1927] suggested a date between 1460 and 1470. The lower part of the painting is missing and also the frame on the right. It is damaged and has been restored.

The Diptych of the Duke and and Duchess of Urbino

On one side are portraits of Battista Sforza and Federico II da Montefeltro, first Count and then Duke of Urbino; on the reverse side are the allegorical triumphs of the pair. The diptych, formerly in the Palace of Urbino, probably in the Audience Hall [Rotondi, *The Ducal Palace of Urbino*, 1950] came to Florence in 1631 as part of the heritage of the Della Rovere, when the ducal line became extinct, and thus to the Uffizi where it now is. To Masselli [in Vasari, 1832] is due its inclusion in the historiography of art, and he dated it not earlier than 1460; Cavalcaselle put the date forward to about 1469, as did Weisbach [RFK 1899], Waters, Calzini [A 1901], Franceschi Marini [RI 1902], and others; while Schmarsow [*Melozzo*, 1885] and Pichi put it a few years earlier, and Witting to directly after 1459. Berenson [1897] put the date forward again to 1465; and Cinquini [CN I, 1905, and A 1906] confirmed this when he published a work by the Carmelite Ferabò — who lived in Urbino from 1465 to 1466 — in which the portrait of the duke is mentioned; and Logan [RA 1905], Ricci, A. Venturi [1911], Graber, Longhi [1927], Focillon, Salmi, Clark, Bottari, and others all agree. In disagreement are Borenius [in Cavalcaselle, 1914], suggesting 1466; Escher [HK 1922], dating it before the Arezzo frescoes; Mather [*History of Italian Painting*, 1923], dating it 1472; Van Marle [XI, 1929,

1459], the year when the duke and duchess were married; Ragghianti [in Vasari, 1949], after 1465. Toesca and above all C.E. Gilbert [M 1941] revived the controversy over the date. As Ferabò's lyric poem mentions only Federico's portrait, these two scholars do not accept identification of the work with the diptych and say that it must have been carried out after the duchess's death (1472), perhaps in 1473; all the more so because — even ignoring A. Venturi's description of Battista's portrait (a waxen death-mask) and perhaps without taking into consideration its state of preservation (see also 22 A) — of the two Latin Sapphic stanzas unde the Triumphs on the reverse side (22, B and D) that relating to the duke seems to refer to the present, while the other refers to some time in the past. L. Venturi has accepted this last thesis, but Meiss [ACHA] convincingly rejects it, and so does Longhi [1962], as it would mean ascribing a different date to *The Brera Altarpiece* (29) in which Montefeltro appears much older. Longhi has remarked that "the unsightly pseudo-Renaissance frame," in which the diptych was inserted in the nineteenth century, separates the paintings and interrupts the original continuity of the landscape, which must have joined behind the two figures facing each other, and certainly behind the two triumphal chariots. As for painting the portraits in profile, this was a courtly tradition rather than due, as Clark suggests, to Pisanello's influence (following in fact the practice of classical medallists); moreover it is known that Federico II was disfigured and had lost

an eye in a tournament, and it was then that his nose was broken. As Longhi points out, the two profiles have a kind of spherical value and the other side of the head is suggested almost by "symmetrical necessity" by the subtle play of their facing each other. The two human forms stand out against the wide landscape with extraordinary truth and atmospheric reality. Panoramic views were numerous, too, in Florentine paintings round about 1460 (in Pollaiuolo, for example) but without, as in Piero, a direct relationship with air and light and the figures in the foreground. The delicacy of the outline of the duchess's head is in contrast with the effect of solid mass in her husband's, accentuated by his hat and because the profile is caught between two zones of similar color: another note of "truth" quite apart from any dwelling on the psychology of character. A comparison is often made with J. van Eyck's *Virgin of the Chancellor Rolin* or *Rolin Madonna* in the Louvre and with Flemish art in general because of the weight given to every detail ("the painting of every inch is a joy to the eye" [Clark]), enriched by Piero's jeweled touch (recalling Watteau [Id.]) and by certain characteristics of the landscape. Unfortunately, as Longhi has remarked, in the nineteenth century the paint was covered with a thick yellowish varnish "which completely altered the tonality, originally much cooler, as can be seen from an area which escaped the varnish."

22 ⊞ ◑ 47×33 ·1465· ▤ ⁝

A. PORTRAIT OF BATTISTA SFORZA
The dark line between the face and the neck (which suggested to A. Venturi the fanciful and rather macabre idea mentioned above) is connected with the style of head-dress (most interesting in the history of costume): it may be a very narrow band or, more probably, a fine strand of hair.

B. TRIUMPH OF BATTISTA SFORZA
On the reverse side of the above portrait. The Sapphic stanza underneath reads: QVE MODVM REBUS TENVIT SECVNDIS/CONIVGIS MAGNI DECORATA RERVM/LAVDE GESTARVM VOLITAT PER ORA/CVNCTA VIRORVM. (She who observed restraint, in success flies on all men's lips, honored by the praise of her great husband's exploits). The chariot is drawn by two unicorns (symbols of chastity) driven by a cupid; in front sit theological virtues; other virtues stand beside the duchess who, seated on a small throne, is deep in a book.

C. PORTRAIT OF FEDERICO II DA MONTEFELTRO
Clark has drawn attention to an "alteration" in the line of the

neck, which was originally longer and perhaps more realistic, while the firm outline accentuates the monumental profile.

D. TRIUMPH OF FEDERICO II DA MONTEFELTRO
On the reverse side of the preceding the text of the Sapphic stanza runs: CLARVS INSIGNI VEHITVR TRIVMPHO/QVEM PAREM SVMMIS DVCIBUS PERHENNIS/FAMA VIRTVTVM CELEBRAT DECENTER/SCEPTRA TENENTEM. (He [Federico] rides illustrious in glorious triumph — he whom, as he wields the scepter with moderation, the eternal fame of his virtues celebrates as equal to the great generals). The duke, seated on a faldstool, is being crowned by Victory; the four cardinal virtues sit at the back of the chariot which is driven by a winged cupid and drawn by two white horses.

The Polyptych of St Augustine

It was painted for the high altar in the church of the Friars of St Augustine at Borgo San Sepolcro, where Vasari mentions it in the same words in the two editions of the *Vite* [1550 and 1568]: "In the convent of the friars of St Augustine he [Piero] painted the picture of the high altar, which was much praised." In 1555, however, the church had been given to the Poor Clares who rebuilt it, reconsecrating it in 1557, while the Augustine friars took possession of the parish church of Sta Maria, demolished in 1771, then immediately rebuilt (1773), and remaining the property of the Augustinian order until 1808. What happened to the Polyptych during this time is not known. It is generally supposed that it was broken up and that at least part of it remained [cf. Busignani] in the first church, on the strength of a quotation from G. Mancini [*Istruzioni . . . di Città di Castello*, 1832] saying that in the "tribune of the nuns" of the church that had become St Clare are "some small panel paintings, some of which from the hand of Piero della Francesca." Perhaps they can be identified with 23 E, F and H; but Davies [1961] draws attention to a later reference to the same panels ("eight beautiful scenes in tempera in which are shown various saints, said to be of the Sienese school and particularly by Jerome of Genga where horses can be seen which Genga loved to paint" [Coleschi, *Storia . . . di Sansepolcro*, 1886]), and therefore Piero's association with them seems somewhat precarious. It is certain that the Sisters removed the Polyptych from the high altar and replaced it with an altarpiece of the Umbrian school (now in the Municipal Art Gallery of Sansepolcro)

having in the center *The Assumption of the Virgin*; and Ragghianti [1949], contrary to other critics, thinks that Vasari's remark refers to this *Assumption*, while Longhi [1927], because of the past tense ("was much praised"), thinks that Vasari referred to a work already dispersed. Milanesi [B 1885] published two documents relating to the Polyptych; in the first, of 4 October 1454, Angelo di Giovanni di Simone d'Angelo — on his own behalf and on that of a deceased brother Simone, and his widow Johanna — wishing to present a *"tabulam que est de tabulis compositam"* (sic.) — to the Augustine Friars, commissioned Piero to paint it, stipulating the use of gold, the type of decoration, etc., that the figures (not specified) must occupy only one side of the whole and that the work must be completed in eight years; moreover there is a reference to another agreement which has not been found. The second known document concerns a payment to the painter on 14 November 1469 and proves the later payment of another sum. As this later sum is also stated, it is usually thought that the work had by then been finished or was nearly complete. Basing his opinion on the subjects portrayed (the treatment of individual details) and on stylistic and iconographical affinities proving a common origin, Meiss [AB] in 1941 suggested that *St Michael* in London (23 B), the presumed *St John the Evangelist* in the Frick Collection (23 C) and *St Nicholas* in the Poldi Pezzoli Museum (23 D) were parts of the Polyptych, and that among the missing parts a *St Augustine* or an *Enthroned Madonna* had formed the center. Longhi [1942], working independently, at the same time came to similar conclusions and also suggested (as having formed part of the Polyptych) the small panels representing *St Monica* and an *Augustinian Saint*, at that time in the Liechtenstein Gallery (23, E and H), another panel of *St Apollonia*, then in the Lehman Collection (23 G), and *The Crucifixion* belonging to J.D. Rockefeller (23 F). Clark [BM 1947] identified a fourth panel in the principal tier of *St Augustine* in Lisbon (23 A). Recently Longhi [1962] disclaimed *St Apollonia*, because he had noticed that the direction of the light was exactly opposite that in all the other panels. According to Meiss, work on the Polyptych was carried on from 1460 to 1470. Longhi thinks that the Frick *St John* is earlier than the last parts of *The Polyptych of the Misericordia* (7, H, I, and J); and that *St Nicholas*, *St Augustine* and *St Michael* — this last similar to work of 1470-80 — followed at different intervals. In regard to the central part, Meiss's hypothesis must be remembered — that a *St Augustine* or a *Madonna* could have held the place of honor; the suggestion of a *Virgin Enthroned* is confirmed by some

22 A (Plate LX)

22 C (Plate LXI)

22 D (Plate LXII)

22 B (Plate LXIII)

steps visible both in *St Michael* in London and in the panel thought to be *St John* in New York. Clark pointed out that in *The Assumption* which took the place of the Polyptych there is a marble balustrade similar to that behind the four principal saints; further, that a painting by Matteo di Giovanni in 1487 — formerly in the church of the Servi and now in the Municipal Art Gallery of Sansepolcro — has an *Assumption* in the center and two saints in each "wing," and if one accepts that these saints are inspired by those in the Polyptych under review, the lost central portion could have been an *Assumption*. After recent restoration of the painting in London, Davies [BM 1967] put forward the hypothesis that the central painting could have been a *Coronation of the Virgin* (see also 23 B) as Levi d'Ancona had already suggested [Catalogue of the Frick Collection, 1955].

The ideal reconstruction of the Polyptych given here can only record the most widely held views of critics. Even if one accepts 23 G, too many details remain unknown for a convincing hypothesis to be put forward.

23   133×60 1465*

A. ST AUGUSTINE
Lisbon, Museu de Arte Antiga
It arrived there in 1936 from Count de Burnay's Collection and was exhibited as by Cima da Conegliano. It was Clark [BM, 1947] who attributed it to Piero and connected it with *The Polyptych of St Augustine* but he asserted that while the master was responsible for the

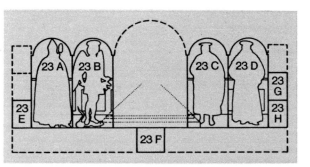

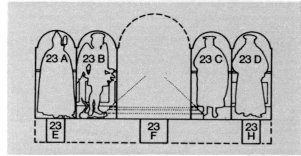

Ideal reconstruction of The Polyptych of St Augustine. *(Above) the supposed structure at the time when it was almost unanimously agreed that* St Apollonia *in Washington (23 G) had originally formed part of the whole. (Beneath)* Longhi's *proposed plan [1963] with the above-mentioned saint excluded and the insertion of the two small Liechtenstein panels (23, E and H) as parts of the predella, together with the* Rockefeller *Crucifixion (23 F) instead of forming part of the side panels of the main tier.*

23 B

23   133×59,5 *1470*

B. ST MICHAEL
London, National Gallery
In one hand the saint holds a scimitar, in the other the head of the dragon whose body he treads underfoot. On his cuirass is inscribed: ANGELVS POTENTIA DEI. LVCHA, preceded by the traces of a "B" (which could also be part of a decorative detail); therefore Meiss [AB 1941] suggests an allusion to Blessed Angelo Scarpetti, buried under the altar for which the Polyptych was executed; another hypothesis by this same scholar concerns the connection with the name of the man who commissioned the work. This would explain why St Michael is referred to as an "angel" instead of an "archangel." In a further effort to explain the mysterious inscription, Meiss suggests a quotation from the Gospel of St Luke. Davies, referring to the overthrow of Lucifer, translates the second and third word — though tentatively — as "by the power of God." Finally Robertson [BM 1953] suggests that the last word was originally "MICHA," the beginning of "Michael," later falsified by some restorer; but radiographic examination shows that this is not so, although the writing has been touched up [Davies, 1961]. The last word induced Cavalcaselle to suggest a collaboration with Luca Signorelli; in this he seems to agree with Clark: an assistant could have done part of the painting, but to distinguish their separate contributions is even more difficult than for *St Augustine* (23 A). The first certain reference to the St Michael panel, after it was separated from the Polyptych, goes back to 1861, when, bearing the false signature of Mantegna, it belonged to the antiquarian Fidanza of Milan. The reference is due to Sir Charles Eastlake, who probably took the picture to England; in 1867 it was placed in its present position. Davies [BM 1967] points out, too, after the most recent restoration, that the step painted in the bottom right hand corner of the panel (similar to that in the supposed *St John* in the Frick Collection

overall design, he only painted the head, the mitre, and the crozier; the rest being by an assistant (not identifiable in any other work by Piero), including the little scenes on the cope, freely adapted from other work by Piero: *The Annunciation* is reminiscent of the same subject in the Arezzo cycle (15 D); *The Presentation in the Temple* goes back to an original from which a banner was designed, variously attributed to Piero himself, to Raphael, to Perugino, etc., and now in the Morandotti Collection in Rome (61); *The Prayer in the Garden* could come from a lost composition in the church of Sargiano, to which Vasari refers (49). Bianconi and Salmi [RDA 1953] agree with Clark, but Salmi thinks that Signorelli was the unknown assistant, at least for the cope. Longhi, on the contrary, describes the little biblical scenes on the cope as "exquisite works" by Piero himself.

23 C

[23 C]) formerly concealed by spurious painting, was originally half covered by some drapery; hence it is possible that the adjoining central panel of the Polyptych showed a *Coronation of the Virgin*, with the figure kneeling on the left. Since the step painted in the Frick panel shows no similar drapery, one might infer the existence of an asymmetrical composition. The saint's face is not in a good state of preservation; some slight "alteration" is visible in the lower part.

23   131,5×57,8 *1460*

C. ST JOHN THE EVANGELIST (?)
New York, Frick Collection
Longhi suggests identifying him with the apostle St Andrew; Davies sees in him St Simon Zelotes, while Meiss [AB 1941] thinks he is St John the Evangelist, with a possible allusion to the father of the man who commissioned the picture and to the latter's sister-in-law (Meiss, without any justification, thinks she married the said Angelo, brother of her dead husband). The figure resembles the saint on the right in *The Brera Altarpiece* (29), identifiable as St John the Evangelist. In fairly recent times the panel was taken from Milan to the collection of Von Miller of Vienna, and from there (1936) to its present position. It seems that in Vienna it was identified by Suida [Longhi]; although it was published only in 1936 by H. Granville [CO]. In regard to the step painted at the bottom left hand corner of the panel, see 23 B.

23   133×60 *1465*

D. ST NICHOLAS OF TOLENTINO
Milan, Poldi Pezzoli Museum
The traditional identification with St Thomas Aquinas has been turned down in favor of the above by Borenius [BM 1916], because the saint wears the Augustinian habit (a determining factor connecting it with the Polyptych under discussion) and the symbolical sun above on the left. A. Venturi [ASA 1893] thought it was St Dominic. Clark thinks

23 D

it possible that the saint's features are those of Giovanni di Simone, the donor. Venturi himself first suggested Piero at a time when it was usually attributed to Fra Carnevale, but later [1922] he attributed it only to Piero's school. Meanwhile Ricci ascribed it to Piero and dated it between 1469 and 1474, as did Berenson [1911]; this opinion has been accepted. In good condition except that the color has been renewed over the right eye and there has been damage and restoration to the hand raised in blessing.

23   39×28 1460*

E. ST MONICA
New York, Frick Collection
Longhi [1942] identified the saint; although at first [1927] he merely rejected A. Venturi's opinion [A 1921] that it was St Clare. It reached its present position fairly recently, together with the following picture, from the Liechtenstein Collec-

23 E

tion then in Vienna. Venturi himself was the first to put forward the suggestion that this saint, and the other painting in the Liechtenstein, were by Piero. Longhi thought it was of the same date as the small circular paintings of saints in the Perugia Polyptych (25, E, F); and he also suggested that they resembled the "little paintings" mentioned by Mancini in the church of the Poor Clares at Sansepolcro (see introduction); on the other hand, they could be those seen by Cavalcaselle in Marini Franceschi's house (42–45). Clark thinks they were painted by a collaborator.

23 F

23 G

23 H

23 ⬙ ⊕ 35,5 × 40,5 1460* 🗎 ⦙

F. THE CRUCIFIXION
New York, J.D. Rockefeller Collection

A. Pope [AA 1917] drew attention to it when it was exhibited at the Fogg Art Museum, Cambridge, Mass. It came from the antique market in Florence (1910–15), having belonged to the Doria Collection in Milan and before that to Prince Colonna in Rome; afterwards it passed from the Duveen Galleries in New York (1924) to C.W. Hamilton of that city and then to its present position. Because of the many removals, Longhi [from 1927 until 1963] and Bianconi thought that there were two separate paintings, one owned by Rockefeller, the other by Hamilton. At first Longhi [1927] confined himself to suggesting only a possible connection with Piero, as he considered some parts "slightly inferior to the master"; then [1942] he decided that it was entirely by him and stated that the "falling off" in quality was due to the restoration carried out in Florence (1910–15). He dated it about 1460 or earlier. Valentiner [*Unbekanntes Meisterwerk*, 1930] thought it a work of Piero's youth, as did L. Venturi [*Italian paintings in America*, 1933]. Clark's opinion is that it was carried out in part by the same assistant who worked on *St Augustine* (23 A).

23 ⬙ ⊕ 41 × 28 1460* 🗎 ⦙

G. ST APOLLONIA
Washington, National Gallery of Art
(Kress Collection)

Before belonging to the Kress Foundation of New York and then the National Gallery in Washington, it was in the collection of P. Lehman and was reproduced in the catalogue by R. Lehman. Longhi's suggestion [1942] that it originally belonged to the little side pilasters of the Polyptych under discussion was unanimously accepted. Longhi, however, [1962] although taking into account that it has the same measurements as the panels formerly in the Liechtenstein Collection (23, E and H), and that it probably came from the Borgo Church of the Poor Clares, excluded it from *The Polyptych of St Augustine* because the light falls on the figure from the opposite direction to that in the other paintings. Instead he put forward the hypothesis that it first of all formed part of a *predella* carried out by Piero in the same church and at the same time as *The Polyptych of St Augustine*. Clark thinks it was painted by a collaborator.

23 ⬙ ⊕ 39 × 28 1460* 🗎 ⦙

H. AUGUSTINIAN SAINT
New York, Frick Collection

At first [1927] Longhi thought this was St Dominic; then [1942] he accepted the above identification which has been generally recognized. For other details see the comments for 23 E.

24 ⊞ ⊕ 1467–68 🗎 ⦙⦙

THE ANNUNCIATION
Arezzo, formerly in the Church of the Santissima Annunziata

On 20 December 1466 (see *Outline Biography*, also for subsequent chronological information) the Confraternity of the Annunciation at Arezzo commissioned Piero to paint a banner of the Annunciation, recommending that "the heads of Our Lady and the Angel be tender and beautiful and of angelic expression." Piero returned to Sansepolcro in 1467 and the following year took refuge from the plague near Bastia. There he painted the standard, received payment for it and handed it over to the Confraternity on 7 November 1468.

The Polyptych of St Antony

The work, composed of nine painted panels (overall measurement 338 x 230 cm.), is in the National Gallery of Umbria in Perugia. Vasari [1568] described it when it was in the Nuns' Convent of St Antony in the same city. Piero also painted the two circular pictures with bust-length figures of saints (see 25, E and F). After Vasari, the work was mentioned by Chiusole [*Itinerario . . .* 1782] and by Mariott [*Lettere pittoriche*, 1788]; in 1810 it was placed in its present position. Cavalcaselle was the first to make a critical examination; he expresses doubts about the authenticity of the three small scenes of the *predella*, then split up, which appeared to him "in a bad state and in great part repainted," so that in reality "they looked like copies and not Piero's original work" (but see below). Berenson at first [1897] recognized Piero's hand only in *The Annunciation*, then [1932] he included the *predella* and attributed the rest to Piero's school. Witting maintained that the whole of the top section was painted independently and was later in date; originally accompanied by the section with the two circular pictures of saints on the *predella* and by an *Epiphany* formerly in the Dennistoun Collection. He also declared that the other parts of the Polyptych attributed to Piero were juvenile works. This supposition was rejected by Weisbach [RFK 1899] and by Aubert [ZFBK 1899] and then by most later scholars. Ricci recognized the work of an assistant, whom A. Venturi [1911] believed to be the same artist who had worked on *The Polyptych of the Misericordia* (p. 87). After Mancini [in Vasari, 1917] had surprisingly suggested 1438 — thinking that Piero had executed the Polyptych with Domenico Veneziano — Longhi [1927] admitted that an unknown painter must have assisted Piero. Longhi linked at least the first paintings for the Polyptych with the Arezzo frescoes, but other parts he thought were painted later. As he had to give an archaic appearance to the work, Piero may have felt it was enough to provide a Gothic frame and a gold background ("it appears evident that the nuns of St Antony wanted a votive painting inspired by the composition Angelico adopted for the polyptych in the chapel of St Nicholas in S. Domenico [now in the same Perugia Gallery] painted for the same city more than twenty years earlier.") Van Marle [XI 1929] favored a late chronology, although he agreed that the work has not survived in its original form. Toesca accepted the *predella* as Piero's work but pointed out affinities with Signorelli in *The Annunciation*. Salmi [1945] dated the whole work just after 1460, and Ragghianti [in Vasari, 1949], and Brandi [*Mostra di Dipinti Restaurati*, 1953], agreed. Clark, who in 1947 [BM] had attributed the design for *The Annunciation* to Signorelli, attributed it to Piero in his monograph of 1951, with the date 1469, and in the assistant who, in his opinion, painted the circular pictures, he recognized the painter of the little saints from *The Polyptych of St Augustine* (23).

Meanwhile, in about 1950, the Polyptych was restored by the Central Institute of Rome [Urbani, BICR 1952]; after this, Brandi [BA 1954] took up Witting's thesis, asserting nevertheless that the whole complex appeared to be the work of assistants (for example, in the central panel, the Virgin's gold brocade garments, certainly Piero's work round the neck, reveal less skillful painting elsewhere), and the working out of the scale for the mount of *The Annunciation* could be original, although the base is narrower than the parts beneath. Ragghianti [in Baldini, 1954] agreed with the reference to the master's youthful activity, except in the case of *The Annunciation*, which he ascribed to 1465. Longhi [1962] has rejected this and thinks that during his maturity Piero agreed to paint an altarpiece prepared for a painter with more archaic leanings, but that the work was conceived as a whole: "the correspondence of the perspective axis of *The Annunciation* with the central cusp of the Gothic triptych [in the principal tier] allows no doubt"; further — the scholar adds — the frame must originally have been rectangular (this is Ragghianti's opinion [see 25 A]) and later cut down in order to adjust it to the other parts, thus clumsily interrupting the architecture of the portico. The general effect of disconnectedness is undeniable. Although one may wish to exclude a great variety of dates, one must accept that the separate parts were carried out at different times between 1460 and 1470 and in the following order: principal tier (where the help of assistants must have been considerable), *predella* (and perhaps the circular paintings), the top section. This hypothesis is suggested by the fact that the two pairs of saints in the principal tier

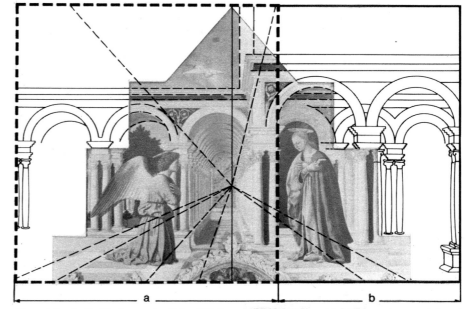

Plan relating to the ideal reconstruction of 25 A according to C.L. Ragghianti's researches, assuming as a working hypothesis the vertical golden section (indicated by the thicker broken line) running along the edge on the right of the column in front of the Virgin. According to this reconstruction the original base of the panel must have been about 225 cm.

appear co-ordinated in space with a more precise reference to the center of the Polyptych than in the Sansepolcro fresco (7), which suggests a rather late period of activity. In *The Annunciation*, the insistence on the perspective "background" seems strange: it is not without affinity — just in those parts which are least convincing — with *The Madonna* of Williamstown (20); moreover the play of light shows similarities with work of about 1470.

25  122×194 *1470

A. THE ANNUNCIATION
C.L. Ragghianti has kindly let us have the results of his research on the probable appearance of the original work. Following the movement suggested by the architecture, the scholar thinks that the side terminals of the painting could be connected with the "gold" in regard to the right hand side line of the column in front of the Virgin; in other words, the outline ought to coincide with the horizontal golden section of the whole panel (that is the segments a and b — as shown in the plan reproduced here — if they were in proportion of about three to two). If this "gold" pivotal hinge be accepted, the line of the pillar is probably correct when the strong contrast between the thin gray of the architecture and the dark tone of the background is taken into consideration. If then *The Annunciation* was mutilated in order, as it seems, to safeguard the external symmetry of the protagonists (simply not to lose any part of it), a center is created which coincides with Piero's practice; one thinks of the Urbino *Flagellation* (11), *The Annunciation* (15 D), and many episodes in S. Francesco in Arezzo (in particular 15, B and H) where the "caesura" towards the center never falls in the exact middle but coincides with the proportion of the golden section, preferably chosen towards the left. The state of the panel, apart from some mutilations, is good.

25  124×62 *1460

B. ST ANTONY OF PADUA AND ST JOHN THE BAPTIST
The halos show — better than those in the twin panel — their mirror-like quality (frequent in Piero [see 17]) and reflect St Antony's tonsure and the Baptist's thick head of hair. The picture is in good condition.

The Polyptych of St Antony *as it appears today. In the upper part, the painting, 25 A [Pls LVI–LVIII]; in the principal tier, 25, B, C and D; below at each end, 25, E and F (see also p. 104); in the* predella, *25, G, H, and I.*

26

25 ⊞ ⊗ 141×65 *1460 ▤ ⦂
C MADONNA AND CHILD, HIS HAND RAISED IN BLESSING
Here, too, the halos are like mirrors and the Child's is marked with a Cross. The form of the base of the throne is arranged so that the two corners, painted in the side panels (25, B and D) fit exactly if the three panels are placed close together. Condition fairly good, in spite of discoloration and missing paint.

25 ⊞ ⊗ 124×64 *1460 ▤ ⦂
D. ST FRANCIS OF ASSISI AND ST ELIZABETH
The condition of the painting is less good than 25 B and the work of assistants more extensive.

25 E

25 F

25 ⊞ ⊗ 21×38 *1460? ▤ ⦂
E. ST CLARE
Sometimes identified with St Rose; but the lilies, the abbess's dress, and the link with the St Francis (in the tier above) make it certain that it is St Clare. The roundel and its pair (25 F) are on the same wooden panel; because of this, it is difficult either to accept or reject the opinion that its original position in the Polyptych is that of today. Recently Clark expressed the opinion that both roundels are wholly from Piero's workshop; but it does not seem reasonable to accept them as less likely to be by Piero than the panels of the principal tier. The state of preservation is good.

25 ⊞ ⊗ 21×39 *1460? ▤ ⦂
F. ST AGATHA
The breasts on a tray are an unmistakable attribute of the martyr. For further details, see the preceding comment.

25 ⊞ ⊗ 36,5×49 *1465? ▤ ⦂
G. ST ANTONY RESUSCITATES A CHILD
Bianconi, publishing an ideal reconstruction of the Polyptych, assumes that there were originally four "scenes" on the *predella*. His opinion derives from the fact that the known episodes relate to St Antony, St Francis, and St Elizabeth, that is, three of the four saints represented in the side panels of the principal tier; thus the scholar thinks that a fourth "scene," now lost, concerned the Baptist (as for the Madonna in the center of that tier, one could accept *The Annunciation* as the complementary "story," or assume that a "story," also lost, was placed between the two roundels). In this case it could have been a *Baptism of Christ*; but Vasari's description — mentioning only three little paintings with "small figures" (see above) — goes against such a theory, unless one assumes that by the middle of the sixteenth century the Polyptych was already dismembered, a fact on which Vasari would hardly have remained silent. In the third painting of the series (25 I), one is aware of the narrative element which Piero does not usually accentuate. Except for a long missing portion on the lower edge, a few horizontal scratches and small abrasions, the condition revealed by recent restoration appears satisfactory.

25 ⊞ ⊗ 36,5×51,5 *1465? ▤ ⦂
H. THE STIGMA OF ST FRANCIS
As in the other two paintings on the *predella*, the artist reveals his skillful presentation of luminous events: here is Piero's second "night scene" after *The Dream of Constantine* in Arezzo (15 E); and this one is no less astonishing than the other in the pallid effect of the landscape which Christ's light seems to cover with snow. Here, too, in no less degree than in the first *predella* painting, the sense of space is at once lyrically apparent. Its state of preservation is the same as in 25 G (see also for other details) except that the empty space at the bottom is more extensive.

25 ⊞ ⊗ 36,5×49 *1465? ▤ ⦂
I. ST ELIZABETH SAVES A BOY WHO HAS FALLEN INTO A WELL
Before the most recent restoration there was some repainting, aimed at "completing" the legs of the man with the anchor, thus altering the balance of the composition. The painting is in worse condition than the other two because of the larger missing area at the bottom and the seriousness of the cracks and the discoloration.

26 ⊞ ⊗ 60×200 *1470*? ▤ ⦂
PERSPECTIVE OF AN IDEAL CITY
Urbino, National Gallery of the Marches
It was connected with three similar paintings in the Staatliche Museen and the Kunstgewerbemuseum in Berlin and in the Walters Art Gallery in Baltimore. They are, however, generally considered of inferior quality except by Berenson, who thought that he could detect to a limited extent the master's hand — and more in the panel in the Staatliche Museen than in the other panels. Other modern critics agree to attribute the work to Piero or simply to unknown Florentine artists). As for the subject, scholars today incline to think it was a "model" for a theatrical scene, accepting moreover information of Mariani, which is by now well worn [*Scenografia Italiana*, 1930], and Krautheimer [*GBA* 1948]. Bianchini [*Memorie . . .*, 1724], perhaps the first to sug-

gest this, connects it with a text of Baldi's [ms. forming part of the Boncompagni Library in Rome, 1587] who referring to the architect Laurana, writes: "That he created beautiful designs and painted skillfully is seen in certain panels on which are colored scenes following the rules of perspective. There is no doubt that they are by him because he has signed his name and written down particulars in the characters and language of Slovenia [that is Slav, as Laurana was a Dalmatian]." These "characters," now no longer legible, would have been apparent in the upper part of the present work, on the façades of the two buildings on the extreme right and left. Cavalcaselle [1864] attributed them to Piero, saying that he remembers the painting in the convent of Sta Chiara in Sansepolcro. Schmarsow [*Melozzo*, 1885] adopted Bianconi's opinion; Von Beber [*SBA*] supported him, asserting that he could read on the panel "VRANNA," to be interpreted as the end fragment of "Laurana." Budinich [*A picture by Luciano Dellauranna*, 1902] agreed (and added to the identification of the writing: "Y" and "LAA" on a scroll, and "AGLA" "147" as well as "VRANNA" in the second), Von Fabriczy [*RFK*

The three works connected with 26. (Above) the panel in the Berlin Kunstgewerbemuseum (arranged as the front of a Renaissance chest) which, according to H. Lehmann [GBA 1936] is an illustration of the Piazza Ognissanti, Florence, while Schubring [Cassoni, 1915] thought it was the St Nicholas Gate in the same city; in any case it is an idealized view. (Center) The Ideal City in the Berlin Staatliche Museen. (Below) the panel in the Walters Art Gallery in Baltimore (where it is attributed to Laurana), in which the idealization is stressed by the juxtaposition of buildings based on those of classical Rome and one inspired by the Baptistery in Florence (towards the right).

1904], Bombe [ibid., 1909], Hutton [in Cavalcaselle, 1909], Kimball [AB 1927] (who put the date forward to c. 1475 on the strength of comparison with Laurana's architectural work), Arcangeli [*Tarsie*, 1942], and Brandi [*Quattrocentisti Senesi*, 1949]. The following critics maintained that the painting was by Piero: Berenson [1897], Witting, Waters, Schubring [*Cassoni*, 1909], Graber [1910], Gronau [T-B 1916] (later [1923], however, he withdrew his opinion and tentatively gave the work to Fra Carnevale), and Escher [HK 1922]. A. Venturi, who first [1911] considered it a work from Piero's studio, later attributed it [1922] to Francesco di Giorgio Martini. Van Marle [XI, 1929], Toesca and Focillon, the last with some hesitation, attributed it to Piero's school. Salmi [1945] dating it about 1470 thought that it derived from Piero; and this seems the most acceptable opinion. Longhi [1927], Baldini, and Bianconi recall it among the works "attributed to" the master; Busignani does not even mention it. Sanpaolesi [BA 1949] cautiously suggests Giuliano da Sangallo. Finally Clark, an obstinate defender of a direct association with Piero, maintains that the marks, or rather the scratchings, visible in the painting were never either Roman or Slav characters; he affirms that the panel was originally the front part of a chest, and notes the Albertian character of the architecture.

27 61×53,5 1470*

MADONNA AND CHILD WITH TWO ANGELS (SENIGALLIA MADONNA)
Urbino, National Gallery of the Marches

It was moved to its present position in the last century from the Church of Sta Maria delle Grazie extra Moenia in Senigallia (hence the name by which it is usually known). Pungileoni [*Elogio ... di G. Santi*, 1822] was the first to mention it, thinking it a sketch for *The Brera Altarpiece* and saying that the angels were portraits of members of the ducal family of Urbino: neither statement has been accepted. In the inventory of the Gallery drawn up by Cavalcaselle and Morelli [GNI 1861] its value was estimated at 2,500 lire: this incredible estimate must have been due to the scholars hesitating whether to attribute it to Piero or to the mythical Fra Carnevale; on the other hand Cavalcaselle confirmed [1864] his own poor opinion of the work by attributing it definitely to Piero's workshop, even if painted under the master's supervision. Anselmi [NRM 1892] attributed it without reservations to Piero, as did A. Venturi [ASA 1893] and later [1911] Berenson, who earlier [1897] had suggested that assistants carried out some of the work. Later critics agree about its authenticity; it has also been agreed

28

ever since Berenson to date it within narrow limits amongst Piero's later works: 1470 according to Longhi, 1472–5 according to Clark. In fact, they discover considerable points of contact with the Perugia Polyptych (25): grandeur achieved without insistence on geometrical simplification, architecture of the type in the Urbino picture (a gray wall, a

niche on the right, a door on the left), a sense of intimacy and at the same time the solving of the problem of space, not by means of measurement, but by varying shafts of light as in Flemish painting. Clark points out that something similar had already been seen in Domenico Veneziano's altarpiece (Uffizi, Florence), as well as in Piero's *Annunciation*

in Perugia: and the origin, according to this scholar, may have been Van Eyck's lost *Lady Bathing* (then in the Collection of the Dukes of Urbino) whose scheme of illumination may have been similar to *The Arnolfini Wedding* in London. The painting underwent restoration at the end of the nineteenth century: after that Anselmi asked that the work be *"rifiorita"* (given a new life) and freed from its "chromolithograph frame"; this was done about 1950 by the Central Institute of Restoration in Rome.

28 124,5×123 1470*

THE NATIVITY
London, National Gallery

Behind St Joseph, who is seated on a rustic faldstool, there are two shepherds; the one on the left appears to be pointing out the prophetic (but here invisible) comet. (Its presence in painting does not seem closely connected with that of the Magi [Davies, 1962²]). In the center, further back, behind the cow, the ass is in the act of braying (experts in iconography rule out any intention of irreverence [Id.]). The landscape is of Sansepolcro [Marini Franceschi, 1912]. The unfinished appearance of the work, which is immediately obvious, is usually attributed to a disastrous cleaning; Longhi denies absolutely that the picture was

not finished, although even recently Robertson [BM 1953] has made this suggestion and Davies is inclined to support him. Some critics identify it with one of the paintings Vasari saw in the possession of Piero's descendants, or rather the descendants of his brother Marco; Giambattista Franceschi, the last of the family, bequeathed it (1698) to his sister Margherita or to her husband, a Marini [RFK 1900]; in 1825 it belonged to a member of the Marini family, perhaps the man responsible for its ruinous cleaning, carried out at the Uffizi in Florence, where it returned about 1848. In 1861 Eastlake mentioned it as being there, and perhaps bought it on behalf of Barker of London; through them it arrived (1874) at the National Gallery. At first [1911] A. Venturi attributed it to the mythical Fra Carnevale, then [1922] to Piero, and this opinion has been accepted. It is also thought to be a late work: Longhi and Clark incline to date it about 1470, Bottari to 1475. Clark lays emphasis on its relationship with Flemish art, both in regard to iconographical elements and in the general tone-color; indeed the Child resembles that by Hugo van der Goes in *The Portinari Altarpiece* in the Uffizi, also of 1475; but Piero's introduction to Flemish painting, specially Roger van der Weyden's, goes back to the

27 (Plate LV)

29 (Plate LXIV)

An illustration of a theoretical plan for 29 according to Ragghianti's researches, based on the identification of the horizontal golden section (indicated by the heavier dotted line). If Ragghianti's hypothesis is correct, the original dimensions of the Altarpiece must have been about 345 × 190 cm.

middle of the century. The strong naturalistic — one might almost say "episodic" — element is Flemish in the description of various details: Longhi notices that Piero attains greater liberty with objects rather than people (so much so that the chorus of angels succeeds in recalling that by Luca della Robbia for the singers' gallery, formerly in the Cathedral of Florence). Moreover, as is usual in Piero, one is not aware of any effort at narration, but rather of a mere presentation of images distributed in space according to an apparently freer metrical arrangement than elsewhere (in several episodes in Arezzo, for example [in particular fresco 15 I]) and yet not less thought out and strict, but with a more subtle, even "cerebral" perspective. Agreement on authorship is based on the color, or rather the light, according to Longhi's fine description in which he notes how the whole structure is "suggested by means of allusions and almost intuitive leaps . . . and the scattered elements bound together and ravished by the sun." One must repeat that in a remarkable manner Piero anticipates Vermeer's luminous silences.

29 ⊞ ⊗ 248×170 ▤⦂ *1472-74*

MADONNA AND CHILD, SIX SAINTS, FOUR ANGELS, AND DUKE FEDERICO II DA MONTE-FELTRO (Brera Altarpiece) Milan, Brera

The saints can be identified as John the Baptist, Bernardino of Siena, and Jerome on the left: Francis, Peter the Martyr, and Andrew on the right. In the last saint but one Ricci recognized a portrait of Fra Luca Pacioli. In 1810 the painting was moved to its present site from the church of St Bernardino in Urbino, where, as early as the eighteenth century, its presence on the high altar was executed in 1472 by Fra Bartolommeo, called there are two references to it: the quotation from Vasari in his biography of Bramante, according to which, as a boy, the future architect studied the paintings of Fra Carnevale in the Urbino district of Sta Maria della Bella; and an entry in the registers of the priory of St Bernardino in the same city, edited by Pungileoni [*Elogio . . . di G. Santi*, 1822] in which it is stated that the painting on the high altar was executed in 1472 by Fra Bartolommeo, called Fra Carnevale of Urbino; and that the Virgin shows a resemblance to the Duchess Battista Sforza and the Child to the young Guidobaldo of Montefeltro. Cavalcaselle, on good grounds, thinks this entry is in eighteenth-century handwriting. It is difficult to relate the work to Vasari's remark and it is probable that he referred to a fairly recent tradition. However, the old reference to Fra Carnevale was accepted not only by Pungileoni and Passavant [*Raffaello . . .,* 1839]

(and at first by Lanzi), but by G.F. Pichi [1892] and A. Venturi [1911], who later [1922] modified his opinion in favor of Piero's school. Cavalcaselle agreed with this last view, as did Berenson [1897] (who later [1911] put forward for the second time the name of Fra Carnevale as the artist responsible for the architectural parts); also Calzini [A 1901], Malaguzzi Valeri [Brera Catalogue, 1908], Hutton [in Cavalcaselle, 1909], Ricci, and then almost all scholars of today. Van Marle [XI 1929] is the only exception. He attributes the paintings of the figures of the Madonna and St John the Baptist, and St Jerome wholly or in part to Signorelli, under Piero's supervision. Cavalcaselle had already pointed out a difference in technique employed in painting Duke Federico's hands compared with the rest of the picture; Frizzoni [*Arte . . . del Rinascimento*, 1891] attributed this difference to fashions borrowed from the series of "illustrious men" in the small study in the Urbino Palace; then Longhi [1927] substituted the name of Pedro Berruguete, certainly working in Urbino in 1477, for that of Justus of Ghent, suggested by Berenson [1911] as Piero's assistant (or the artist who carried on his work). Longhi, too [1963], thought that the assistant had painted the helmet in front of the kneeling duke; and this opinion is shared by many. The Altarpiece is usually dated between 1469 and 1475; only Rotondi [BEA 1947] suggests a later date because of the presence of St Bernardino, and L. Venturi dated it definitely 1483, that is, after the death of Federico II. The painting is certainly a votive offering and could have been commissioned for the church of S. Bernardino on the occasion of the birth of Guidobaldo da Montefeltro

(1472); it could not have been finished later than 1474, because the duke is not wearing the Order of the Garter bestowed on him that year. Such are M. Meiss's conclusions [SDCG, and AB 1954]. He also [ACHA] comments on the meaning of the ostrich's egg hanging from a chain in the apse, which could be a Christian symbol of the four elements (according to several references to the subject in medieval literature) and a symbol of creation (it usually has this meaning when suspended in Abyssinian churches and in those in the Christian East). The allusion to Guidobaldo's birth would therefore be evident. His mother, Battista Sforza, died in the same year and was buried in S. Bernardino. The egg also recalls the Renaissance idea of perfectly centralized, harmonious, and symmetrical space.

The high altar of S. Bernardino was strictly related to the architecture of the church; it echoed its rhythms and the harmony was absolute between the figures and their surroundings. Clark thinks that the architecture in the picture may have been derived from Alberti's designs for S. Andrea in Mantua, and that in this, apart from the egg, consists its fascination; otherwise, as regards the figures, it reveals in Piero a "loss of pictorial appetite"; rather a curious criticism, which contrasts with Longhi's expression of sympathetic understanding: "It is uncertain whether the architecture has dictated the arrangement of the human beings or whether they have not dictated the arrangement of the architecture." There is nothing further to add, except to stress the importance the composition had on Venetian painting, from Antonello to Giambellino and those who followed them. Ragghianti [in Baldini, 1954]

30

states that the Altarpiece was soon multilated on every side and that in its original form it must have been "framed by lateral pillars in the foreground (the projecting edges of cornices can still be seen) and by an arch against the light." Ragghianti has kindly given us a plan (reproduced here) of the ideal composition for the painting. In this case, as in the Perugia *Annunciation* (see 25 A), the starting point, in order to discover the original size of the work, is a search for a harmonious balance, based, in the present case, on the division between the group of figures and the "empty space" above; in particular, the golden section on the line — parallel with the base of the picture — cutting across the top of the Madonna's head determines (taking into account the plan of the architecture suggested by the details which have survived) the original development towards the top and the bottom. For the restoration of the sides, apart from the integration of the figures at the extreme right and left, the architectural structure functions as a guide in the upper zone. The credibility of the general scheme thus planned finds support in the fact that the egg hanging above the throne is the geometrical center of the complete composition; confirming the absolute symmetry beloved by Renaissance artists. The hypothesis about the cutting down of the altarpiece is proved by further examination carried out by the Gallery's staff.

30 ▦ ◉ — 63×55 ▤ ⦂

MADONNA AND CHILD (MADONNA VILLAMARINA)
Rome, Villamarina Collection (on loan to the Galleria Nazionale d'Arte Antica)
When the picture belonged to the marquises of Azeglio it was exhibited (1865) as a work by

33

Piero at the British Institute in London. It then went to Villamarina. Already in 1864 Cavalcaselle had judged it rather a poor work by an Umbrian follower of Piero's. L. Venturi [A 1905] expressed the opinion that it could be a work of Piero's youth, when he was with Domenico Veneziano; Ricci agreed and dated it 1441-4. But A. Venturi [1911]

attributed it first to Fra Carnevale, only to change [1922] and attribute it to Piero della Francesca's school, as did Gronau [T-B 1916], Toesca and Grassi [1945]. Berenson [AA 1926], comparing it with the *Madonna* in Boston and that in Oxford, formerly believed to be by Piero (55 and 63), was convinced it was painted by Signorelli in his youth, as were Van Marle [XI 1929], Clark [1951], and Salmi [*Signorelli*, 1953]; while Ragghianti [in Baldini, 1954] attributed it to Giovanni Santi. Also Longhi [1927] (declaring it the work of an unknown follower) and Bianconi both exclude it from Piero's work.

31 ▦ ◉ — *1474 ▤ ⦂

FRESCOES
Sansepolcro, formerly in the Badia (Chapel of the Madonna)
Known only because of the note of payment on 12 April 1474 (*Outline Biography*). One may suppose that they illustrated the life of the Virgin and were begun — or work on them was in progress — during the previous year, when it is definitely known that Piero was in Sansepolcro (ibid.).

32 ▦ ◉ — 1478* ▤ ⦂

MADONNA
Sansepolcro, formerly in the Hospital of the Misericordia
Commissioned in 1478 by the Confraternity of the Misericordia at Borgo for frescoes on a wall "below the church and the hospital" aforesaid [Milanesi, in Vasari, II, 1878]. Corazzini [*Appunti . . . su la Valle Tiberina*, 1875] thought he had discovered it, but the authorship he proposed had been rejected by Cavalcaselle.

33 ▦ ◉ 41×27,5 1478-80? ▤ ⦂

PORTRAIT OF GUIDOBALDO DA MONTEFELTRO (?)
Lugano, Von Thyssen Collection
It belonged to Dennistoun, who [*Memoirs of the Dukes of Urbino*, 1851] said he had bought it in Urbino from G. Crosti. The historian, thinking it a portrait of Raphael painted by his father Giovanni Santi, arranged to have it restored. Still attributed to Santi, it was moved in 1934 from the Hirsch Collection to that of Von Thyssen-Bornemisza. In the catalogue, however, it is attributed to Melozzo da Forlì and, after recent restoration (1963), to Piero della Francesca, at Hendy's suggestion. This critic accepts it as a portrait of the young Guidobaldo da Montefeltro (suggested by Zeri), and dates it between 1478 and 1480. Hendy also suggests a comparison with the Duke and Duchess of Urbino in the Uffizi Diptych (22) which is difficult to accept; all the more so because the above chronology does not fit in with Piero's development.

Other works mentioned in original sources

The works listed here are mentioned in original records and attributed to Piero della Francesca, but as no chronological information is given it is impossible to fit them into the *Catalogue*. The list, in alphabetical order, gives the place where the painting was executed or where it was last mentioned.

ANCONA

34. THE MARRIAGE OF THE VIRGIN
In the church of St Ciriacus, "on the altar of St Joseph" Vasari mentions a "Marriage of Our Lady," and C. Posti [LM 1907] puts forward some hypotheses on the possibility of its having been a fresco, etc.

AREZZO

35. ST VINCENT
Vasari remembers "a St Vincent in a niche" in the parish church of St Bernardino.
36. ST DONATUS WITH ANGELS
Vasari also remembers in the church of Sta Maria delle Grazie "a St Donatus in full pontificals with some cupids." (See 53).
37. ST BERNARDINO
In the first edition of *Le Vite* [1550] Vasari mentions "a St Bernardino on a column" in the parish church; this reference is omitted in the second edition [1568].

BOLOGNA

38. WORKS ON AN UNKNOWN SUBJECT
Pacioli [1509] remembers some paintings by the master but gives no details.

LORETO

39. WORK OF AN UNKNOWN SUBJECT
In the Sanctuary Vasari refers rather vaguely to Piero beginning a fresco "with Domenico da Vinegia in the vault of the sacristy" which was finished by Signorelli. If the remark is true (Signorelli's help in finishing it seems unlikely) the work must have been carried out in about 1438, when it is known that Domenico Veneziano was in Umbria (*Outline Biography*).

PERUGIA

40. WORKS ON AN UNKNOWN SUBJECT
Without later on giving any details, Vasari records that there were "many things" by Piero in Perugia towards the middle of the sixteenth century.

PESARO

41. WORKS OF AN UNKNOWN SUBJECT
Both Pacioli and Vasari refer in general terms to Piero's work in this city.

SANSEPOLCRO

42-45. FOUR SAINTS
Cavalcaselle and Milanesi [in Vasari, II, 1878] remember the busts of four saints in Marini Franceschi's house. A. Venturi [A 1921], Longhi [1927], and others identify them with those formerly in Liechtenstein, and connected with *The Polyptych of St Augustine*; but these same scholars think it more likely that the saints came from the choir of the nuns' church of Sta Chiara in the same city (see 23, E and H).
46. SELF-PORTRAIT (?)
Cavalcaselle and Milanesi both mention a presumed self-portrait of Piero in Marini Franceschi's house. It is thought to be a copy of the one used by Vasari as the frontispiece of his biography of Piero [1568]. The painting [RA 1920], formerly belonging to the above family, is today in the town hall in Sansepolcro (see p. 83), and is now usually ascribed to Santi di Tito and

painted at the end of the sixteenth century.
47-48. TWO SAINTS
Vasari describes as "very beautiful two saints in fresco" by Piero "inside the middle door of the parish church."

SARGIANO (AREZZO)

49. THE PRAYER IN THE GARDEN
Vasari mentions that in a chapel in the church of S. Francesco is a "Christ praying in the Garden," and describes it as "the most beautiful work of the master." G. Piacenza [in Baldinucci, *Notizie*, II, 1770] states that "one can still see a part."

URBINO

50. WORKS ON AN UNKNOWN SUBJECT
Vasari refers to "many most beautiful pictures of small figures which in the city of Urbino have come to grief during numerous wars suffered by that State." One might suppose that among them were *The Flagellation* and perhaps *St Jerome and a Worshiper* (11 and 3).

Works formerly attributed to Piero della Francesca

Of the various works ascribed to Piero, especially between the end of the last century and the first decade of our own, those most reliably attributed to him are listed here. Many "pieces" ascribed to Piero have, however, been omitted if they have been attributed to him as the result of private surveys and without serious philological examination.

AREZZO

51-52. THE PRAYER IN THE GARDEN and THE RESURRECTION OF CHRIST
Cavalcaselle [VIII, 1898] saw them in the Funghini Collection and judged them to be by Piero. Falciai [Arezzo, 1910] referring only to the first "small painting" merely remarked that "many attribute it to Piero della Francesca." The attribution for both paintings was rejected by Longhi [1927], in agreement — it would seem — with Van Marle [XI 1929] who, however, while mentioning them as being in the above collection,

said he had not seen them. Later criticism is silent about them.

53. STORIES OF ST DONATUS
In a place adjoining the church of Sta Maria delle Grazie, A. Melani [AS 1904] and U. Tavanti [A 1906] trace various fragments of frescoes which originally must have decorated the loggia formerly surrounding the vast piazza in front of the church. Some of these fragments relate to a fresco on whose lower frieze one can read "Siranna," which makes one think of the subject was *St Donatus giving Sight back to Siranna*. Tavanti, while admitting much help from Piero's workshop (especially, perhaps, from Lorentino d'Arezzo) thought he recognized "here and there, the pearly colors of Piero's canvases." On a nearby wall "in an absolutely ruined condition" he thought he could make out traces of "St Donatus in pontificals, sitting on a chair drawn in perspective, with some cupids,"

53

54

mentioned by Vasari (see 36), but hardly identifiable from the fragments "of the perspective, a few folds of a mantle and the outline of a cupid's bare leg." Berenson (after 1909 [*Central Italian Painters . . .*] although admitting the intervention of some assistants), Ricci, Falciai [*Arezzo*, 1910], and others accepted the direct reference to the master; but A. Venturi [1913] and Longhi [1927] firmly rejected it in favor of Lorentino d'Arezzo, supported with hesitation by Van Marle [XI 1929]. Successive scholars do not mention the matter; and in fact it cannot be accepted as Piero's work.

BAYONNE

54. THE REDEEMER BLESSING
The panel, painted in tempera [Gruyer, GBA 1903, and Musée Bonnat, 1908], belongs to the Musée Bonnat. Gruyer appears to accept the traditional opinion that it is by Piero. According to Longhi [1927] it belongs to the Venetian school of about 1460. The work is spoilt by large damaged areas and old restorations.

55

BOSTON

55. MADONNA AND CHILD AND AN ANGEL
The panel (59 × 41 cm.) was transferred in 1923 to the Museum of Fine Arts. The attribution to Piero, confirmed by A. Venturi [1922], was rejected by Berenson [AA 1926] in favor of Signorelli. Later [1932, 1936, etc.] he was more definite, saying it was a juvenile work of this artist from Cortona. Salmi [*Signorelli*, 1953] agreed with him. Modern critics do not include it among Piero's works.

56

CITTÀ DI CASTELLO

56. THE REDEEMER BLESSING
It is in the Municipal Art Gallery. Berenson [*Central Italian Painters*, 1897] suggested that it was a late work by Piero and he repeated this in the last edition of the *Indici* [1953], but this is considered doubtful. In Longhi's opinion [1927] it is by a Flemish painter who imitated Piero and Justus of Ghent; but Van Marle [XI 1929] rejected this and suggested that it was by a direct follower of Piero's.

57

FLORENCE

57. MALE FIGURE
It forms part of *The Crucifixion* frescoed about 1360 by Orcagna in the refectory of the Priory of Sto Spirito. Ragghianti [CA 1954] suggested that it was a juvenile work (1439) by Piero which was added to the fresco, on which Gentile da Fabriano had also worked in about 1420. This

59

60

thesis was rejected by Salmi [1955] and by Longhi [1963] (he declared it "inadmissible on technical grounds"), nor did Bianconi accept it.

NEW YORK

58. PORTRAIT OF A WOMAN
The panel (58 × 38 cm.), having belonged to the Toscanelli family [Catalogue, 1883] and to the Aynard family [Catalogue, 1913], went to the Lehman collection. On the back is written: "Portrait of Battista Sforza, wife of Federigo, Duke of Urbino. Died 1473" and "by the hand of Piero della Francesca." Today it is thought that only the cataloguers of the Aynard Collection mistook it for a work by Piero. Berenson, having at first attributed it to Antoniazzo Romano [*Central Italian Painters*, 1911], in the editions of *Italian Pictures of the Renaissance*, from that of 1932 to the last one of 1953, though with doubts, changed his mind and attributed it to Piero. In Lehman's opinion [Catalogue, 1928] the portrait was by Paolo Uccello. L. Venturi [*Pitture Italiane in America*] agreed (dating it 1468) and so did various other critics; though Offner [BM 1933], Pope-Hennessy [*Paolo Uccello*, 1950], and later scholars, while attributing it to some artist in

58

Paolo's circle, incline rather to the "Master of the Nativity of Città di Castello." The latest criticism favors Domenico Veneziano or an artist closely associated with him.

59. THE TRIUMPH OF FAME (or OF CHIVALRY) (?)
This roundel belongs to New York's Historical Society. Berenson suggested that it was by Piero [GBA 1905 and 1906]; März immediately opposed it [RA 1907] in favor of the school of Domenico Veneziano. It was ignored by later scholars, including Berenson.

OXFORD

60. MADONNA AND CHILD AND THREE ANGELS
The panel (86 × 57·8 cm.), painted in tempera, belongs to Christ Church, who received it as a gift in 1828. The attribution to Piero is claimed by Witting, Waters, and some other scholars at the beginning of the twentieth century. At first Berenson [1911] thought it was by Bartolomeo della Gatta, while Venturi [1913] inclined to Fra Carnevale; meanwhile Fry [BM 1911] and Borenius [id., 1916] favored Piero's circle and Venturi himself [1922] agreed, as did the cataloguers of the exhibition of Italian art held in London in 1930. Berenson [AA 1926] had proposed attributing it to Signorelli and dating it about 1465 and he supported his idea in successive *Indici* until that of 1953 without convincing scholars that it was the work of this artist from Cortona. Salmi [*Signorelli*, 1953] suggests that it may have originated in Lippi's circle.

ROME

61. THE PRESENTATION IN THE TEMPLE
The canvas (178 × 135·6 cm.) — moved from Doughty House (Richmond) to the Cook Collection of Richmond, then to Agnew's in London and finally to A. Morandotti in Rome —

61

was painted as a processional standard, and because of this the tempera is somewhat faded. In 1909–10 it was exhibited in Burlington House, London, as a work by Marco Marziale, while Gnoli [RAU 1910] attributed it to Lorentino d'Arezzo. Van Marle [XI 1929] agreed and discerned in it one mediocre painting by an artist working with Piero della Francesca. Geiger [JPK 1913] accepted the attribution to Marziale, and Berenson gave him some support. Although including it in the catalogue of Piero's work, he said that it could indeed be a copy of Marziale. Borenius [Cook Catalogue, 1913] ascribed it to Piero's school, and L. Venturi [*Italian Paintings in America*, 1933] to Raphael's youth. Zeri [BA 1953] qualified this opinion and attributed it to Perugino as an early work, and Camesasca agreed [*Tutta la Pittura del Perugino*, 1959]. After Van Marle had drawn attention to some points of similarity with early works of Signorelli, especially as regards the Virgin's figure, although the technique is coarser and the impasto heavier than is usual in the Cortona painter's work, Salmi [*Signorelli*, 1953] associated it definitely with early work by Signorelli, and indicated an echo of Piero in the proportion of the columns (other reminders of the master are revealed in the types chosen for the Madonna and the man carrying a roll of parchment as well as in the lamp hanging before the niche in the background [Camesasca]). Ragghianti believes that it is by Giovanni Santi (see 30).

62. HEAD OF A YOUNG WOMAN
It belongs to the Gualino Collection. The attribution to Piero is to be found in all Berenson's most recent *Indici* (up to that of 1953), but no other scholar has agreed with him. The bad state of the picture makes a reliable judgment impossible.

Appendix Piero della Francesca as draftsman and writer of treatises

Because of the impermanence and fragility of drawings made during most of the fifteenth century, the sheets on which Piero must have carried out sketches, studies, and other initial research have disappeared; and the little that is attributed to him concerns work formerly — and even now — believed to be by others. This consists of two single sheets, both in the Cabinet of Design and Engraving in the Uffizi in Florence (see below), both of superlative quality; but modern critics have not yet had an opportunity of deciding whether they can be definitely attributed to Piero.

His enterprise as a theorist is amply documented, as has been pointed out *(Critical History* and *Bibliography).* We are not concerned here with his treatise *Del Abaco,* dealing mostly with mathematical calculations and other "subjects . . . necessary for merchants," but will concentrate on two books directly concerning the decorative arts: *De Prospectiva Pingendi* and *Libellus de Quinque Corporibus Regularibus;* particularly the first, about "measurement which we call 'perspective'" which, with "drawing" and "coloring," form the basis of painting; indeed — and the subject was of vital importance

to artists of the Renaissance — Piero goes so far as to identify perspective with painting itself. The problem had been confronted by Ghiberti, Brunelleschi, and Alberti; but in comparison with their intuitions and codifications a noble originality inspires Piero's text. By applying the strict rules of geometry he achieved in the modern sense the interpretation of the concept of space in scientific terms rather than in the metaphysical terms of ancient perspective [Olschki]. He raised perspective to the realm of ideas in which Galileo's genius was to work to such fruitful purpose [Bottari]. For Piero the perception of natural objects becomes manageable if they can be brought back to the essential and measurable regularity of geometrical forms: the world exists for him in so far as one can define its proportions. The treatise is divided into three parts: perspective of flat figures, perspective of solids (mazzocchio, column, human head, etc.), perspectives of the same bodies according to the practices of the studio. That is to say, it does not deal with systematic theorizing, but with exercises, graded according to difficulty, thought out to enable the reader — particularly the

painter — to solve every problem; or to equip him with a body of instructions to enable him to plan the composition of the "stories" which he will transform into painting [Nicco Fasola]. And these instructive diagrams were highly appreciated by a whole group of artists and theorists — the German Dürer, the Frenchman Jean Pélerin, the Venetian Daniele Barbaro, the Bolognese Sebastiano Serlio — who, in their turn, made use of them in their own treatises.

The *Libellus* concerns the doctrine of the "regular" bodies, relating to the harmonious construction of the human body, letters of the alphabet, etc., as well as of columns and other architectonic elements. This was the work that brought Piero the greatest, but not the most lasting fame; it was for this reason that Luca Pacioli [1509] plagiarized it, as Vasari pointed out, Egnazio Danti [*Due Regole della Prospettiva Pratica,* 1583] denounced it, and Leopoldo Cicognara [*Catalogue Raisonné . . .* 1821] supported it; and as was hardly believed for a long time, even after Jordan [1880] had compared Piero's text (traced to the Vatican Library by the scholar himself) with that of brother Luca.

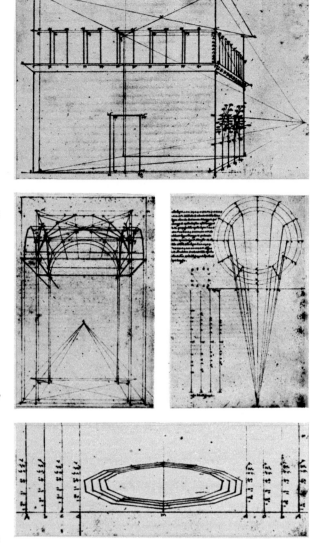

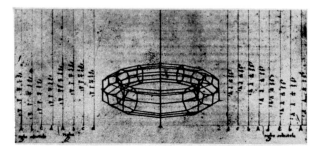

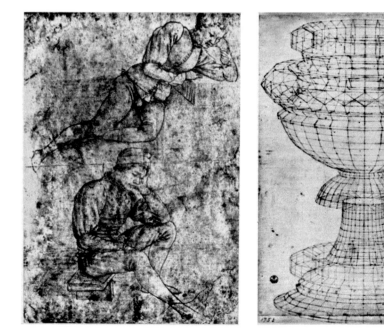

Here, above and below, are some original drawings by Piero della Francesca, illustrating De Prospectiva Pingendi. *There is no dispute about their being genuine; not even modern critics have expressed doubts. The sketches executed by the master are either in a manuscript in the Ambrosiana Library in Milan, containing the Latin version (with numerous corrections in Piero's hand, though the text is by an unknown hand) or in the Palatine Library in Parma with the Italian version. Nicco Fasola has remarked that the latter shows it has been frequently consulted, the former rather less; but the Italian version has more mistakes (specially reversed letters) than the other. It seems that the author worked more diligently on the Latin version for the use of learned scholars (who, however, must have consulted it seldom); while the Italian text, in spite of misprints, found a great number of readers, specially amongst painters for whom it was written.*

(Above) *Sketch for the perspective of a building, one of the first eleven theorems proposed by Piero as a means of expressing the "flight" of the ground floor and the building constructed on it.* (Second row) *perspective of a chapel on a square ground plan and an intermediary stage in the "degradata" construction of a "torculo" (see below) similar to that carried out by Paolo Uccello in the well-known perspective studies on the "mazzocchio" (Uffizi, Florence).* (Third row) *similar construction to the one above but less complicated.* (Below) *final operation in order to obtain the perspective of a "torculo . . . having eight circles comprising the size [in relation to the thickness] in twelve equally divided parts."*

(On the left) *The figures of two young men (pen and sepia on white paper, 370 × 290 mm.; Florence, Uffizi); Van Marle, XI, 1929; Berenson, 1938; Sabatini, 1944; Ortolani, 1948, etc., judged them to be of Antonio Pollaiuolo's school. Grassi [Disegni Italiani in 1300 and 1400, no date] attributed the drawing to Piero (perhaps a copy of an unknown original by the artist). (On the right) A Study in Perspective of a Vase (pen on white paper, 340 × 240 mm.; ibid.); usually attributed to Paolo Uccello because of Vasari's allusion to the "mazzocchi and points and bosses" that the Florentine painter loved to draw; on the other hand Parronchi [Studi su la Dolce Prospettiva, 1964] thinks that it is by the Master from Borgo and that Vasari's remark "a vase represented [by Piero], by means of squares and faces" refers to it. Parronchi points out that the vanishing perspective is very slight and comprehends not only the depth of the vase but its height, also that the image makes actual the "rational triumph over matter, the sublime coincidence, never raised to this degree, between poetry and abstraction."*

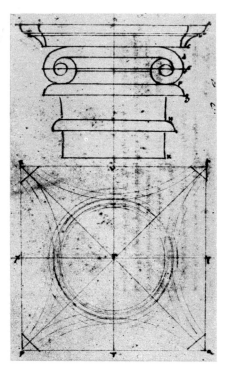

On this page, too, are drawings by Piero for De Prospectiva Pingendi. As in the preceding page the sketches are reproduced according to the original order of the theorems to which they refer (except in the case of the third and fourth illustrations – from the top – to the right on p. 109, which have been changed over to fit in with the arrangement of the text on the page). Preference has been given to sketches illustrating genuine problems in perspective (which in the text of the treatise begin with theorem XIII in the first book, continuing with the remaining seventeen, with the twelve in the second book and with the same number in the third and last book) omitting those relating to the first twelve theorems which concern optical-geometrical premises (from I to VII) and the purely geometrical (from VIII to XII) as the foundation of the treatise on the perspective of the ground plan and the buildings erected on it.

(On the left, at the top) the drawing refers to the preliminary phase for the perspective projection of an Ionic capital. (In the center) design illustrating an intermediary stage for the perspective drawing for a Corinthian capital. (Bottom) illustration for the last phase of the same theorem. Capitals similar to this one can be seen in the Urbino Flagellation (11) and in two episodes in the cycle in S. Francesco at Arezzo (15, B and D).

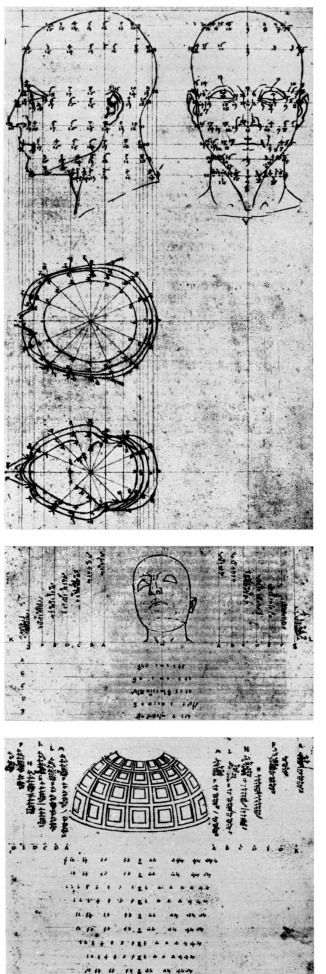

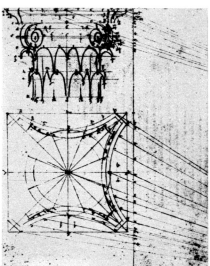

(On the right, at the top and in the middle) drawings illustrating the theorem that "proportionately the head gradually diminishes": the upper drawing shows the first stage, the projection of circles round a human head: the other shows the problem solved. Heads vanishing in perspective like this last are illustrated in The Polyptych of the Misericordia (7 H) and in The Resurrection at Sansepolcro (19); the very ones thought to be self-portraits (see p. 83). (At the bottom) one of the drawings relating to "measuring a dome scientifically" (detail). A similar apsidal cupola, enriched with rosettes, finishes off the throne on which the Madonna and Child are sitting in the central panel of the Perugia Polyptych (25 C). The final connections between Piero's sketches for De Prospectiva and his paintings have not been settled. If by any chance a building resembling that reproduced on the preceding page can be identified with Perspective of an Ideal City of Urbino (26) in the Piero della Francesca circle, and with the wells in the foreground of the same picture, it can perhaps be due to the drawing illustrating one of the first stages for the perspective of a "torculo" reproduced on p. 109.

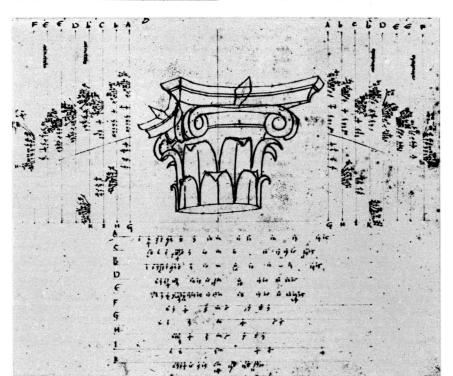

111

Photographic sources

Color plates: Cooper, London; Marques, Lisbon; National
Gallery, London; Scala, Florence; Staatliche Museen,
Berlin.
Black and white illustrations: Bullatty-Lomeo, New York;
Museum of Fine Arts, Maria Antoinette Evans Fund,
Boston; Rizzoli Archives, Milan; Scala, Florence, Soprin-
tendenza alle Gallerie, Florence; Walters Art Gallery,
Baltimore.
Graphics by Sergio Tragni.